P9-EEC-908

DANTE'S DIVINE COMEDY

PURGATORY

Journey to Joy, Part Two

DANTE ALICHIERI

Dante Alighieri
Gustave Doré

DANTE'S DIVINE COMEDY

PURGATORY

Journey to Joy, Part Two

Retold, with Notes, by

Kathryn Lindskoog

Read Dante. . . .
Down to the frozen centre, up the vast
Mountain of pain, from world to world,
he passed.

C. S. Lewis

MERCER UNIVERSITY PRESS
MACON, GEORGIA
1997

Mercer University Press
6316 Peake Road
Macon, Georgia 31210-3960
© 1997

The paper used in this publication meets the minimum
requirements of American National Standard for Information
Sciences—Permanence of Paper for Printed Library Materials,
ANSI Z39.48–1984.

Jacket art:

Library of Congress Cataloging-in-Publication Data

Lindskoog, Kathryn Ann.
Dante's Divine Comedy/ Purgatory, retold, with notes,
by Kathryn Lindskoog.
p. cm.
Includes bibliographical references.
Contents: v. [1]. Purgatory. Journey to joy, Part two
ISBN 0-86554-573-1 (alk. paper)
1. Dante Alighieri, 1265–1321—Adaptations. I. Dante
Alighieri, 1265–1321.
Divina Comedia. English. II. Title.
PS3562.I5125D36 1997
813'.54—dc21
97-4270
CIP

MUP / H401

Contents

Frontispiece   ii

Dedication   vi

Preface   vii

Acknowledgments   viii

Botticelli's "Primavera" and Dante's *Purgatory*   ix

Purgatory   1

Epilogue   199

Further Reading   200

PREFACE

To read Dante is a joy.
To write about Dante is a pleasure,
for it is impossible to write about him
without reading him again more closely...
Etienne Gibson

People visit ancient cathedrals for all kinds of reasons. Some marvel at them because they are almost supernatural feats of engineering genius. Others go to contemplate marvelous stained glass windows. Some are intrigued by fascinating sculptures. Some spend days studying the tombs and their inscriptions. Some attend concerts there. Many explore cathedrals out of curiosity, and others have merely ducked inside to escape the weather. Some go because it's the thing to do. Some people know all the terms and what they mean: naves, apses, transepts, flying buttresses, facades, portals, wings, piers, vaults... Others know none of the terms, but thrill at the beauty. A few look at a cathedral as a gigantic stone history book.

Some go there to worship.

Reading Dante's *Divine Comedy* is much like visiting a cathedral. Visitors who try not to miss anything in a cathedral are apt to defeat themselves because it is too much, and readers of Dante who try not to miss anything also defeat themselves. There is far too much to take in at once.

To begin with, *The Divine Comedy* was written in rhymed poetry, not plain prose, and in Italian, not English. C. S. Lewis said that Dante is the most translatable of poets, but this guide is not exactly a translation. It is a faithful sentence-by-sentence restatement of Dante's spectacular Italian poetry in today's clear English prose (based on the work of many translators), for the sake of the story that Dante has to tell us about our journey to joy.

Many love Dante best as an Italian poet. Some love him as a spokesman for the medieval world. Some love him as a philosopher. Some love him as a builder of intricate intellectual systems. Some love him as a critic of the Medieval Church.

But those who love him best as a Christian storyteller and spiritual teacher for all people may say this book is the glimpse of Dante we have been waiting for.

ACKNOWLEDGMENTS

Thanks first to Dorothy L. Sayers, who is my chief guide through Dante. Thanks also to John Ciardi, Allen Mandelbaum, Mark Musa, contributors to the Carlyle-Wicksteed edition, and other translators. Thanks to the many world literature students who have ventured through Dante's mysterious realms with me. Thanks to my invaluable translation consultants in Italy, Vicki and Valerio Bernardi. Thanks to Ranelda Hunsicker, kindliest of encouragers. Thanks to Marc Jolley, the Dante lover at Mercer University Press who met me midway on my journey to publication and guided me there. And to my husband John, who deserves at least a canto of terza rima, I can only say thanks for everything.

This book is dedicated to Father David Baumann and the Church of the Blessed Sacrament, Placentia, California.

BOTTICELLI'S "PRIMAVERA" AND DANTE'S *PURGATORY*

For centuries the most famous and popular illustration of Dante's *Divine Comedy* has remained "lost," although during the past hundred years millions have seen it and admired it.

Sandro Botticelli painted "Primavera" ("Allegory of Spring") circa 1478 as a huge (roughly 6' by 10') wall decoration for the elegant home of a young member of the Medici family. Although it is painted on a wood panel, the design is much like that of a medieval tapestry. It is one of the most beloved treasures of the Uffizi Gallery in the heart of Florence—in spite of the fact that its meaning remains a puzzle to art experts as well as the general public. It appears to depict an odd mixture of figures from ancient Greco-Roman mythology.

In fact, the supposedly inexplicable picture is primarily Botticelli's depiction of Dante's sacred Garden of Eden in *Purgatory*, Cantos 28-31. Thus "Primavera" is not just a mysterious and melancholoy tribute to paganism after all. It is an intentional Christian allegory as orthodox and ultimately joyful as John Bunyan's *Pilgrim's Progress*.

Set apart in the center like a serene but childless Madonna, Dante's beloved Beatrice presides benevolently over the tableau, adorned with a cloak of red and a patterned halo of sky light. Her right hand gestures acceptance just as Mary's does in Botticelli's "Annunciation." (Art critics identify her as an unusually circumspect Venus, goddess of love and beauty.) At Beatrice's left hand her friend Matilda has been gathering wildflowers as in Canto 28. (Most critics identify her as Flora, goddess of spring, who is scattering flowers.) At

Beatrice's right hand three maidens, Hope, Faith, and Charity, dance in a circle as in Canto 30. (Critics identify them as the Three Graces, daughters of Zeus.) The luminous equanimity of Beatrice and her four friends is paradisaical. Dante's leafy canopy spreads overhead, and his carpet of grass and flowers spreads underfoot. As Matilda says, "Here spring is everlasting."

Like the center panel in a triptych altarpiece, this happy central scene is flanked by two related scenes. On the far right a disheveled Eve lurches vulnerably, with a broken sprig dangling from her mouth. (In Canto 29 Dante deplores Eve's primordial disobedience in the Garden.) Eve is being steered and perhaps propelled toward Adam by a winged Satan, who hovers in some trees with his garment curving like a large snake. (Critics often identify Eve as the nymph Chloris, and Satan as the West Wind.) Critics note a general sense of movement from right to left in "Primavera," and that tallies with the movement of the divine pageant in Canto 29 from east to west. (The viewer of "Primavera" is in the same position as Dante the pageant viewer.)

On the far left a jaunty, casual, unfallen Adam gazes up and reaches as high as fruit on a nearby tree. (In Canto 28 Matilda deplores Adam's loss of this happy Garden full of laughter and play, which was a foretaste of eternal peace.) According to Genesis, Adam was not only the first man and the first resident of Eden, but also Eden's caretaker, the first agriculturist. This figure probes even higher with a rod that has become obscure because the painting is darkened by old varnish and the upper left part is especially dark. There are several possibile meanings for the rod.

I can't help suspecting that Adam's costume is meant to suggest Mars (the god of war), not Mercury (the god of commerce) as critics assume. This figure lacks Mercury's characteristic wings on his hat and sandals. His helmet, boots, and sword are appropriate for Mars, and he resembles the Mars in Botticelli's "Mars and Venus." Because he was the unfortunately appropriate city god of Florence, Mars had special significance for Dante, Botticelli, and the owner of "Primavera." Dante's visit to the Garden of Eden takes place in March, the month of Mars and the beginning of Spring. Most significant of all, in my opinion, Mars was originally the Roman god of agriculture and fruitfulness rather than war; thus he is a highly appropriate figure in an archetypal garden. And if his rod is a magic wand with which he dissipates clouds, as many critics believe, that might be an allusion to the power of Mars over agriculture.

As a literate Christian, Botticelli was almost surely familiar with the Old Testament symbolism for war and peace. Joel 3:10 speaks of beating plowshares into swords and pruning hooks into spears. Perhaps Botticelli had the dual role of Mars in mind when he made it clear that the lower parts of some of the trees near the sword bearing figure had been trimmed by a garden caretaker. If so, he no doubt had Micah 4:3-4 in mind also: "They will beat their swords into plowshares and their spears into pruning hooks. Nation will not take up sword against nation, nor will they train for war anymore. Every man will sit under his own vine and under his own fig tree, and no one will make them afraid, for the LORD Almighty has spoken" (NIV). This famous passage expresses human longing for the Edenic state portrayed so memorably in "Primavera." On the other hand, if the figure in question really represents Mercury rather than Mars, more commentary about that aspect of the allegory would be welcome.

Like a whimsical afterthought, Cupid floats above Beatrice at the very top center of the picture with his blindfold on and his dangerous unaimed dart ready to fly, as mentioned by Dante in Canto 28. But Cupid was not an afterthought; he represents the central theme of Dante's entire *Comedy*, which is that humans are born to be in love with God and to move ever closer to Him, but their love goes astray when they become so enamored of lesser delights that they don't find out what their deepest yearning is really for. Furthermore, in Canto 31 four maidens remind Dante that when he had first looked into the eyes of Beatrice, Cupid had aimed his arrow at Dante. (That symbolic arrow is what eventually led to Dante's salvation.)

Like Dante's poetry, Botticelli's art was extremely lyrical and popular, and also intellectually sophisticated. Why should Botticelli have depicted eight of Dante's Garden of Eden figures as a random assortment of stock figures from classical mythology? This surface ambiguity is an exuberant kind of applique that Botticelli imposed upon his tableau to reflect the fashionable Neoplatonism of the owner of "Primavera" and his like-minded friends; they enjoyed relating elements of Christianity to classical mythology. (In a sense the happy patron got two paintings for the price of one.) This was done in the spirit of Dante, a master of dexterity, double meanings, and extraordinary synthesis.

This tour de force may have been inspired by Canto 31 of *Purgatory*, There Dante stared into the eyes of Beatrice and was amazed to see a stationary image of Christ somehow change back and forth, back and forth, from human to divine. I suspect that the original purpose of the dual nature of "Primavera" was to create an earthly analogy to that image, in which one painting would have two natures: one human (classical mythology), and the other divine (Christian allegory).

Perhaps Botticelli was studying and illustrating Dante before he was commissioned to create "Primavera." Until almost 1460, all books were handmade and very expensive. Thus it was a literary landmark when a relatively inexpensive edition of *The Divine Comedy* came off the press on August 30, 1481, produced by the very group of Florentine Neoplatonists who had been connected with the creation of "Primavera" about three years earlier. This book was illustrated with engravings based upon sketches commonly attributed to Botticelli. In 1976, art historian Sir Kenneth Clark claimed that those illustrations were designed by Botticelli and that he was working on them early in the 1470s.

Forty years after Botticelli's death, art critic Giorgio Vasari (architect of the Uffizi Gallery) not only claimed that Botticelli produced those designs, but that he also wrote his own commentary on parts of *The Divine Comedy*. Scholars assume that Vasari was in error about the commentary, as he often was about other topics; but Botticelli's brother Simone, who lived with him for many years, owned an unsigned manuscript of a *Divine Comedy* commentary. (Could it possibly be by Botticelli?) That manuscript exists to this day in the National Library in Florence.

Although critics don't think Botticelli wrote a commentary on Dante, many of them think he painted the portrait of Dante that resides in Switzerland. And everyone agrees that he was a Dante enthusiast. According to Sir Kenneth Clark, Botticelli studied the leading Dante commentary of his day, and one of his friends was a great Dante scholar.

In 1492 an Italian navigator discovered America. Right about then the owner of "Primavera" commissioned the artist to return to *The Divine Comedy* and illustrate it from beginning to end without any overlay of Greco-Roman mythology. On beautiful white parchment he produced a large illustration for each of the 100 cantos and at least one extra; but only ninety-two are known to survive, and most of those were not completely finished. Only a handful were even partially colored.* They were much admired when they were new; but the sheepskin had been wrongly prepared, and only faint ghosts of the wonderful drawings remain on the parchment. So it is that the only enduring public legacy of Botticelli's great love for *The Divine Comedy* is the world's beloved "Primavera."

---

* A detail of Botticelli's most complete and enduring illustration on parchment can be seen on the cover of *The Divine Comedy: The Inferno, Journey to Joy.*

CANTO ONE

 Down to the Dewy Grass

Now the little ship of my story-telling talent hoists her sails to glide across better waters, leaving behind that cruelest sea.[1] And I will sing about a second kingdom, in which the human spirit is cleansed and becomes ready to go on up into heaven.[2]

Here, sacred muses whom I serve, let my poetry revive; and let Calliope accompany me from afar with the sweet music that once vanquished the nine daughters of King Pieros and turned them into magpies.[3]

The sweet blue of eastern sapphire, spreading on the clear forehead of the sky all the way to the serene horizon, restored joy to my eyes as soon as I emerged from the deathly air which had polluted my eyes and heart. The planet that is linked with love was making the East laugh

---

[1]*Purgatory* is generally considered the easiest part of *The Divine Comedy* to read and assimilate. It is longer than *The Inferno*, but to many readers it seems shorter.

[2]*Purgatory* is more like spiritual life on earth than *The Inferno* and *Paradise*. As G. K Chesterton pointed out, *The Inferno* is Dante's vision of failure and *Paradise* is Dante's vision of perfection, but *Purgatory* is his vision of improvement. The structure of *Purgatory* is divided into three parts: Cantos 1-9, entering Purgatory; Cantos 9-27, the journey up Mount Purgatory; and Cantos 28-33, the entryway to Paradise.

[3]Dante begins *Purgatory* with a traditional epic appeal to the creative muses for inspiration. In mythology Calliope was the muse who inspired epic poets, and she was foolishly challenged to musical competition by the daughters of King Pieros.

with light, outshining the Fishes that swam in the sky below her.[4]

I turned to my right, set on seeing the southern pole, and saw four stars never seen before except by the first pair of humans. All heaven seemed to rejoice in their fire. O northern hemisphere, you are like a widow without the sight of those stars![5]

When I finally stopped gazing at them, turning a bit toward the northern pole where the Wain constellation had already sunk below the horizon, I saw near me an ancient man with a noble countenance that called forth as much reverence as any son could owe his father. His beard was long and flecked with silver, like his hair that flowed down on both sides to his chest. The four holy stars were lighting his face with such radiance that I saw him as if the sun had been shining on him.[6]

"Who are you who have come up along the dark stream to escape from eternal prison?" he said, shaking his venerable head and swaying his long hair. "Who guided you? Or who was your lamp when you issued forth from the deep night that will always keep that hellish valley black? Can the laws of the pit be broken? Or is there some change of plans in heaven that allows you, being damned, to come here to my stony slope?"

Then my guide laid his hands on me and with a few words, nudges, and gestures had me show reverence with bent knees and bowed head.

---

[4]The planet Venus was shining in the East, along with the Pisces (fish) constellation.

[5]These are spiritual stars, not features of ordinary astronomy. They will appear again to Dante as four maidens in Cantos 29, 31-33.

[6]In Cantos 29 and 31 Dante identifies these four stars as the four cardinal virtues (common to pagans and Christians) which all other virtues depend upon: common sense, justice, courage, and self control.

Then he answered, "I did not come on my own. A lady came down from heaven and prayed for me to accompany this man. But since it is your will to know more about our situation, it can't be my will to refuse. He has never yet seen his last hour, although through his madness he came so close to it that there was little time left for him to turn around. As I said, I was sent to rescue him, and there was no other way but the way I chose. I have shown him all the guilty people, and now I want to show him those spirits in your keeping who are cleansing themselves.[7]

"How I brought him here is a long story. A power from above enables me to guide him here to see you and hear you. Now may it please you to be gracious about his arrival; he seeks freedom, which is precious — as anyone knows who gave up his life for freedom. You know, because for freedom's sake death was not bitter to you in Utica, where you left your earthly garment that on that great day will shine brightly.[8]

---

[7]Dorothy Sayers makes six extremely important points about Dante's Purgatory. (1) No soul in Purgatory can go to Hell; they are all on their way to Heaven. (2) Purgatory is not an afterlife chance to turn to God; to get there the soul must have already chosen God. (3) Even a last-minute deathbed movement of the soul toward God will suffice to get a soul into Purgatory. (4) The greater part of a soul's purification should take place on earth; but when that does not occur, it takes place in Purgatory. (5) People on earth can bless those in Purgatory with their prayers; but any attempt at communication with souls in Purgatory is wicked. (6) Some souls are ready to enter into the presence of God immediately upon death, without Purgatory; these are the saints, usually known only to God.

[8]Virgil realizes that the noble pagan guarding the mountain is Cato of Utica, a Roman born in 95 B.C. An opponent of Caesar's rule, he committed suicide in 46 B.C. rather than endure imprisonment; in his culture this represented supreme devotion to liberty. Virgil indicates that Cato will receive a glorified body on judgment day, but this does not mean that he will ever enter into heaven. He is an inhabitant of

"We don't violate the eternal laws, because he is alive and I am not a prisoner of Minos. I come from the circle where the pure eyes of your Marcia are. There she prays to your blessed heart to count her as your own. For her sake, then, let us go through your seven kingdoms. I will take back to her my gratitude toward you, if you allow your name to be spoken below."

"Marcia was so pleasing to my eyes when I was on the other side," he answered, "that I did anything she asked. But now that she lives beyond the evil river, the law about my coming here decrees that she cannot sway me.[9] But if a heavenly lady sends you and directs you, there is no need for flattery. It is enough that you ask me in her name.

"Go on, and be sure to fasten a smooth reed around his waist, and wash his face so that all filth is wiped away; because it is not fitting for any eye clouded by mist to go before the first angel on duty here from Paradise.[10] The shoreline of this little island, beaten by waves, grows reeds in the soft mud. No leafy or stiff plant can live here, that fails to bend with the buffeting.

"But do not return this way. The sun is rising, and it will show you an easier way to climb this mountain." Then he vanished.

I arose without speaking and joined my guide, with my eyes on his face. He began, "Son, follow my steps. We are turning back to go down the slope to sea level." The

---

Limbo who has been posted just outside heaven. He represents pagan virtue and duty.

[9]Marcia was Cato's wife, and here she symbolizes human virtue. Because Cato is now oriented toward heaven, he is responsive to heaven's will rather than to the demands of human virtue. (This does not mean that there is any conflict between the two.)

[10]In *The Faith of Dante Alighieri* Geoffrey Nuttall says of *Purgatory*, "I know of no other work the total effect of which is at once so cleansing and so renewing."

dawn was triumphing over the morning darkness, which fled before her, so that in the distance I recognized the trembling sea. We strode along the lonely plain like one who is returning to his lost path and until he reaches it counts his time wasted. When we had reached a place of breezy shade where dew resists the sun, my leader spread both hands upon the sweet grass. Being aware of his purpose, I raised toward him my tear-stained cheeks. There he uncovered the true color of my face, which Hell had coated over.[11]

Then we came to a deserted shore where no one ever sailed away and then returned. There to please another he bound my waist. What a wonder! Just as he picked a humble reed, it was replaced instantly where he had torn it away.[12]

---

[11]Dorothy Sayers says, "Before ascending the Mountain, Dante's face must be cleansed from the tears he shed in hell. The penitent's first duty is cheerfulness: having recognized his sin he must put it out of his mind and not wallow in self-pity and self-reproach, which are forms of egotism."

[12]Dorothy Sayers reminds readers that Dante's rope belt was thrown into the pit in *The Inferno*, Canto 20, to call up the monster Fraud. Dante's new belt is made out of a pliable, yielding reed, which symbolizes humility. Both Virgil and Dante are now humbly pliable and yielding. Humility is a key element in *Purgatory*.

The Celestial Pilot
Gustave Doré. (Canto 2)

CANTO TWO

Glad Ship of Singing Souls

By now the sun must have been sinking below the western horizon of that far hemisphere with Jerusalem at its center, where from the sands of the Ganges night was rising with her Scales constellation, which drops in autumn. In contrast, where I was the pink and white cheeks of Aurora, goddess of dawn, were quickly turning yellow with age.[1]

We were still standing beside the sea, like people pondering their path — whose bodies linger while their hearts are already on the way. Then, just as sometimes in early morning the red light of Mars burns through the mist low over the western sea, I saw a light (God grant that I may see it again!) speeding over the ocean faster than any other kind of flight.

When I looked back at it after glancing at my teacher in hopes of information, it was already brighter and larger. On each side of it I saw something white, and then below it something white gradually appeared. My teacher still said not a word, until the first pair of whitenesses looked like wings and he recognized the pilot.

"Bend, bend your knees!" he cried. "Behold the angel of God! Clasp your hands. You will see more angels from now on.[2] Look at how he needs no human tools, so that he

---

[1] Dante and Virgil are on an island in what is now called the South Pacific, straight through the earth from Jerusalem.

[2] Many angels appear to Dante in *Purgatory*. In his essay "Imagination and Thought in the Middle Ages" in *Studies in Medieval and Renaissance Literature* (Cambridge: Cambridge University Press,

uses no oar or sails except his own wings to travel between distant shores. See how he has them pointing to the sky, piercing the air with eternal feathers that never shed like temporary plumage."

Then as the divine bird came closer and closer, he became so bright that my eye could not endure it. I cast my eye downward, and he came to shore with a vessel so swift and light that the water covered none of it.

On the stern stood a heavenly pilot with blessedness written all over him, and inside there sat more than a hundred spirits. They all sang together in one voice, "When Israel went out of Egypt" and the rest of that Psalm.[3] Then he made the sign of the Holy Cross, and at that they all leaped onto the shore; and he left as quickly as he had come.

The crowd that he left there seemed unfamiliar with the place and gawked like one who is seeing new things. On every side the sun, who with his bright arrows had chased the Goat constellation from the center of the sky, was shooting forth the day.[4] Then the new people looked at us and said, "If you know the way up the mountain, show us."

Virgil answered, "You probably think that we are familiar with this place, but we are strangers here like you. We arrived just a little while before you, by a way that

---

1966), C. S. Lewis describes the natures of nine classes of angels as understood in the Middle Ages. "It is this conception, as well as the poet's own genius, which gives Dante's angels a sublimity and masculinity never captured in later art."

[3] They are singing Psalm 114 in the words of the Latin Vulgate, "*In exitu Israel de Aegypto.*" Israel's escape from slavery in Egypt serves as a symbol of the souls' escape from death into life.

[4] The Goat constellation is Capricorn.

was so rough and hard that this further climb will seem like play."[5]

The souls who noticed my breathing realized that I was still alive, and they turned pale with shock.[6] Just as a crowd desiring news will press toward a messenger carrying an olive branch,[7] and none hang back from the jostling, so all those fortunate souls stared at my face as if they had forgotten to keep moving toward their future beauty.

I saw one of them move forward to embrace me with affection, and so I responded in the same way.

What an empty mirage! Three times I reached around him with a hug, and pulled my hands to my own chest. I think I must have flushed with confusion. The shadow smiled and drew back, but I flung myself toward it. Gently it motioned me to wait. Then I recognized him and begged him to stay a while to talk to me.

He answered, "Just as I loved you when I was in my mortal body, so I love you now that I am free, so I will stay. But why are you here?"

"My dear Casella, I am taking a journey in order to get back here again some day. But how have you lost so much time getting here?"[8]

He answered, "I am not wronged if he who carries away when and whom he pleases has many times denied

---

[5] In *The Inferno* Dante was shy about using Virgil's name, but now as their affection grows he calls Virgil by his name occasionally.

[6] Just as the appearance of a spirit can shock a living person in this world, the appearance of a living person can shock a spirit in the next world.

[7] A messenger used to carry an olive branch to show that he had good news.

[8] Casella was a musician who had set some of Dante's poems to music. He had been dead long enough that Dante was surprised he had not arrived in Purgatory sooner. The Pope had declared 1300 a year of Jubilee, easing the way for people who died that year.

me this trip, for his will is shaped by the Just Will. For three months now he has been easily taking on board all who want the trip. Therefore, at the seashore where the Tiber becomes saltwater, I was gathered in.[9] Right back to that river mouth he has set his wings again, because those who do not sink down to River Acheron are always assembled there."[10]

I said, "If no new law has removed your memory and mastery of the songs of love that used to satisfy my longing, then may it please you to comfort my soul awhile, which is weary from coming all this way with my body."

"Love, in my mind speaking to me," he began so sweetly that the sweetness still echoes within me.[11] My teacher and I and the people with him seemed entranced with pleasure. We stood still, hanging on every note; and then the noble old man cried, "What's this! Dawdling spirits! What negligence, what tardiness is this? Hurry to the mountain and strip yourself of the scabs that prevent you from seeing God!"

---

[9] It is only those who feel ready and willing who choose to take the trip. Geoffrey Nuttall points out in *The Faith of Dante Alighieri* (p. 17), "In Purgatory and in Heaven it is recognised on all hands that the journey, with all it reveals, is owing solely to God's goodness, generosity, and grace. The strangeness and the marvel remain; but God's grace is always strange and marvelous..."

[10] The souls that were bound for Purgatory assembled in Rome at the mouth of the Tiber River and were ferried by an angel; those who were bound for Hell assembled by the River Acheron and were ferried by a demon. The angel used his wings, and the heavenly boat flew; Charon used an oar to paddle and sometimes hit his passengers with it. The blessed souls were singing in unison; the damned were wailing and cursing separately.

[11] This is one of Dante's own poems, which Casella had no doubt set to music for him. We have the poem in Dante's book *Convivio*. A major theme in *Purgatory* is learning not to let earthly loves distract us from heavenly love.

Like a flock of pigeons that are feeding on wheat or tares, all quietly absorbed in their feast and not preening and strutting in their usual way—if they see something they fear, they instantly desert their food because this is more urgent. That is how I saw the newcomers drop the song and start for the mountain, like a person who rushes off before he gets his bearings.

And we left just as fast.

CANTO THREE

A Flock of Timid Sheep

Their sudden flight scattered the souls across the meadow, toward the mountain where justice scours us clean. But I stayed close by my faithful companion, for how could I have made good time without him? Who else would have brought me up the mountain?

He seemed to be gnawed by self-blame. To such a clear and noble conscience, how sharp is the sting of a minor slip![1] When his feet had forsaken the haste that temporarily robbed him of his dignity, my mind—which was deeply absorbed[2]—eagerly broadened its focus, and I looked toward the hillside that soars most steeply from the sea toward heaven. The light from the sun that was flaming red behind us was broken before me because sunbeams were resting on my body.

When I saw that the ground was dark before me alone, I spun around in terror that I was abandoned.

Then my comforter faced me and said, "Why do you distrust me again? Don't you believe that I am with you to guide you? It is already evening there where my body that made a shadow lies buried. (Naples possesses it because it was moved from Brindisi.)[3]

---

[1] In *The Figure of Beatrice* Charles Williams points out that in *The Inferno*, Canto 30, Dante lingered to listen to obscenities, and here Virgil has lingered to listen to a love song. In both cases the traveler realizes he should not have been delayed by the distraction.

[2] Dante was absorbed in Caselli's song, in Cato's rebuke, and in his own part in both.

[3] It is late in the day in Italy when it is early morning in Purgatory. Virgil's body was moved from Brindisi to Naples by the order of

"If I cast no shadow, be no more surprised than when you see that the heavenly spheres don't block each other's light. The Power has arranged for bodiless bodies to be able to suffer torments, heat and frost; but how this is done, He does not choose to tell us.[4] Only a madman hopes that human reason can understand the infinite road traveled by one Substance in three Persons. Limit yourselves, you of the human race, to discovering what is. For if you had been able to understand the why of everything, there would have been no need for Mary to give birth.[5] And you have seen wise men of old longing without hope, whose longing can't be satisfied and causes them eternal grief. I'm talking about Aristotle and Plato and many others."

At that point he hung his head and said no more and seemed dejected.[6]

By this time we reached the foot of the mountain and found a cliff so steep that nimble legs were useless. The most desolate, jagged stretch of cliff between Lerici and Turbia is a wide, easy staircase in comparison.

My teacher halted and said, "Now who knows where the mountain slopes so that a person without wings can go up?" He looked down, searching his mind about what to do, and I stood looking up the rock wall.[7]

Augustus, and the tomb that allegedly holds his body can still be seen on the road to Pozzuoli.

[4] All the souls (bodiless bodies) that Dante had observed in Hell could somehow suffer physically although they were not physical and would have cast no shadow if the sun had reached them.

[5] It was the dissatisfaction of Adam and Eve with knowing *what is* without *why* that led to the fall of humankind and the need for redemption through Christ.

[6] Virgil is one of the "many others" in Limbo who are doomed to exist forever without hope of rejoicing with God in Heaven. They and their bright hopeless castle were described in Canto 4 of *The Inferno*.

[7] According to medieval calculations, Dante's Mount Purgatory is over 3,000 miles high.

To my left I saw a group of souls walking toward us, and yet they moved so slowly that they didn't seem to get any closer.

"Teacher," I said, "look up. Over there is someone who may give us advice, if you don't have any advice for us."

He looked up and answered gladly, "Let's go to meet them, because they come so slowly; and you keep up your hope, dear son!"

When we had gone about a thousand steps and the people were still about as far off as a good thrower could pitch a rock, they all pressed close to the steep cliff and stood frozen the way a terrified man will stop and stare around in dread.

"You whose life ended well, you spirits who are already chosen," Virgil began, "by that same peace which awaits you, tell us where the mountain slopes so that we can climb it. For those who know most about the value of time are frustrated most by lost time"[8]

Just as sheep come out of the pen in ones and twos and threes, and the others hang back timidly with their nose to the ground, and what the first one does the others do also, huddling close behind, silly and silent and not knowing why—so I saw the first of that fortunate flock come toward us, looking meek and dignified. When the first ones saw the sunlight split apart on the ground to my right, so that my shadow ran to the rock, they stopped and drew back a bit; and all those that followed did the same without knowing why.

"Without your asking, I confess to you that this is a human body you see which splits the sunlight. Don't be astonished, because it is only with power from Heaven that he seeks to surmount this wall." So said my teacher.

---

[8]There is a sense of eager hurry in Purgatory.

And those good people answered, "Turn around then, and enter before us." With a backhanded gesture they waved us on.[9]

Then one of them said, "Whoever you are, as you move forward turn and consider if you ever saw me over yonder."

I turned and looked hard at him. He was golden-haired and fair, with noble features; but one of his eyebrows had been split by a wound.

When I had humbly denied ever seeing him before, he said "Now look," and he showed me a wound high on his chest. Then with a smile he said, "I am Manfred, grandson of Empress Constance. I pray that when you return, you go to my fair daughter, mother of the kings of Sicily and Aragon, and tell her the truth in case she has heard otherwise.[10]

"After my body was pierced by two fatal stabs, I gave myself up, weeping, to Him who willingly forgives. My sins were horrible, but infinite goodness has such wide arms that it welcomes all that turn to it.[11]

"If Cosenza's pastor, who was sent by Clement to chase me down, had read well this page of the book of God, the bones of my body would still be at the bridgehead near Benevento under the guard of heavy

---

[9]In *The Faith of Dante Alighieri* (p. 42) Geoffrey Nuttall points out that one of the characteristics of Purgatory is the ubiquity of helpers. "Even in Heaven (where, it is true, this is less necessary) we are not aware as we are in Purgatory of being surrounded by helping hands, of ministering spirits all about us."

[10]Manfred wants his daughter Constance to realize that he is in Purgatory, not Hell.

[11]Manfred was the natural son of Emperor Frederick II and was reportedly even more self-indulgent than his father. He was a musician and singer with great style and courtesy, and he always wore green. He lived as a generous and popular lover of pleasure. As Dante would have known, Manfred was accused of murdering his father, a brother, and two nephews.

stones. But now the rain washes them and the wind stirs them, beyond the banks of the Verde where he carried them with unlit candles.[12]

"Such a curse is not strong enough to deny to a man a return of eternal love, so long as there is the slightest green sprig of hope.[13] It is true that he who dies in rebellion against the Holy Church and then repents at the end must stay down here for thirty times as long as he spent in rebellion—unless good prayers on earth reduce the wait.

"You see how glad you can make me if you reveal to my dear Constance that you have seen me, and the length of my delay.[14]

"You people there can help us to advance."[15]

---

[12]Manfred, who had been excommunicated for opposing Pope Clement IV, was killed at the Battle of Benevento in 1266. Near there the victorious Charles of Anjou buried him (correctly, in unconsecrated ground) and caused all his soldiers to file past and pile rocks over his body as a protective tribute. But the archbishop of Cosenza moved the body outside papal territory entirely, with unlit candles as a sign of condemnation.

[13]Alan Jones points out in *The Soul's Journey* (p. 117), "We live in hope because in purgatory things move; history is malleable. Dante's whole life as reflected in his poem is the radical reinterpretation of his own history in the light of the revelation of God's love, which holds everything in being. We know that hell is not remedial--there can be no pursuit of lost alternatives--but the vision of hell is renewing and full of hope."

[14]Geoffrey Nuttall points out in *The Faith of Dante Alighieri* (p. 11), "The spirits in Hell are still concerned for their own reputations on earth... The concern of the spirits in Purgatory is different. They beg Dante on his return to earth to speak of them that not their reputation but the truth about them may be known on earth. Otherwise, their only desire is that those on earth should pray for them, thus assisting their present cleansing."

[15]Those who have to wait a long time in Purgatory do so in confident hope, not misery.

The Ascent
Gustave Doré. (Canto 4)

CANTO FOUR

Up a Cranny in the Cliff

When one of our five senses receives great pleasure or pain, the soul is completely focused there and seems to give no heed to anything else. This disproves the mistaken belief that the body has more than one soul. That is why when the soul is fascinated by something that is seen or heard, time slips away without our noticing. For our awareness of the passage of time is not like an awareness that fascinates us. The former awareness is weak, and the latter kind is overwhelming.

I had a genuine experience of all this while listening to that spirit and marveling. The sun had climbed up a full fifty degrees[1] and I had not noticed it, by the time we came to where those souls cried out to us in unison, "Here is what you want!"

Often when his grapes are darkening with ripeness, the peasant will close a small gap in his hedge with a little forkful of thorns. It was a narrower gap than this that my leader started to climb, with me after him, just the two of us, when the flock of souls left us.

One can walk up San Leo and clamber down to Noli.[2] One can climb to the summit of mount Bismantova with

---

[1]The sun climbs 15 degrees every hour. The sun had arisen at 6 A.M., and when it was 50 degrees above the horizon, the time was about 9:30 A.M.

[2]San Leo was a small town perched upon a ridge in Urbino. Noli was a little town that could only be reached by sea or by climbing down steps cut in the rocks above it.

feet alone. But here a man had to fly—I mean with the swift wings and pinions of immense desire—behind the leader who gave me hope and was my light.

We were climbing within the cranny in the rock, wedged in on both sides and gripping the path with both hands and feet. When we had reached the top of that stone cliff, out on an open bank, I said, "My teacher, which way shall we take?"

He answered, "Don't take any steps aside; keep climbing up behind me until we find some trusty guide." The summit was so high that I couldn't see it, and the slope was far steeper than a forty-five degree angle.

I was exhausted when I cried, "Sweet father, turn and look at how I'll be left behind if you don't stop."

"My son," he said, "drag yourself that far," pointing to a ledge a little higher up, which ringed that side of the mountain. His words spurred me on, and I forced myself, crawling after him, until the terrace was under my feet. There we both sat down, facing the east from which we had come; for looking back usually gives people cheer.

First I set my eyes on the seashore below, and then I raised them to the sun; and I was amazed that it fell upon us from our left. The poet was quick to notice that I was astounded to see the chariot of light moving between us and the far north.[3]

Therefore he said to me, "If the constellation of Castor and Pollux were near that mirror[4] that reflects light up and down, you would see the glowing Zodiac revolve

---

[3]Because Dante and Virgil were in the Southern Hemisphere and facing eastward, the spring sun was northward and to their left. (If they had been back home in Italy in the Northern Hemisphere and facing eastward, the sun would have been southward and to their right.) Dorothy Sayers says, "Readers in Australia, New Zealand, and South Africa will find that (for once, in a European literary classic) the Sun is in the right part of the sky."

[4]The sun is like a mirror reflecting the light of God.

closer to the Bears, unless it went off its old track.[5] If you want to imagine how that can be, figure that Mount Zion in Jerusalem and this mountain are opposite each other through the earth, with exactly the same horizon ringing their two opposite hemispheres. So it is that the sun's path, which Phaeton followed so poorly,[6] passes this mountain on the north and Mount Zion on the south."

"Certainly, teacher of mine," I said, "I never grasped it so clearly as I do now, although I was a bit slow to catch on. The line scientists call the equator, which has the sun on one side and winter on the other, is exactly as far north of here as it was toward the warm south from where the Hebrews lived.[7]

"But if you don't mind, I would like to know how far we have to go, because this hillside soars higher than my eyes can reach."

He answered me, "This mountain is always difficult at the bottom where one begins, but the higher a person climbs, the easier it gets. Therefore when it becomes as easy to you as floating downstream in a boat, you will be

---

[5]If it were the season when the Twins (Castor and Pollux) constellation were close to the sun, the sun would be even closer to the Bear constellation—even farther north.

[6]In mythology, Phaeton, son of Apollo, begged to drive his father's chariot, the sun, and almost destroyed the earth with his bad driving.

[7]Geoffrey Nuttall observes in *The Faith of Dante Alighieri* (pp. 9-10), "...the story Dante tells is tied firmly to earth and earthly reality. Technically, one may say, this is simply the artistry which casts verisimilitude over narrative and commands a willing suspension of disbelief. For narrative so peculiar it is, surely, great artistry. But Dante's purpose and the effect which he achieves are much more than this. The serious reader-- and Dante writes for no other--soon perceives that the story is eminently serious because the writer believes it to be in principle true for Everyman and intends the reader to find life or death put before him."

at the end of the climb. There you will be able to rest. That's all I have to say, and I know it's true."[8]

When he had said this, a voice nearby said, "Perhaps before then you might need to sit down!" At that we spun around and saw on the left a boulder that we had not noticed before. We went toward it and saw people lounging in the shade behind the stone, slumped lazily. One of them, who looked fatigued, was sitting with his arms around his knees and his face down between them.

"My sweet sir," I said, "take a look at the one who looks as if Sloth were his own sister."

Then that one turned and looked at us, lifting his face just above his thigh and saying, "Climb on up, if you're that energetic."

Then I knew who he was, and my shortness of breath did not stop me from going right to him. After I got there, he slightly lifted his head and said, "Have you figured out how the sun drives his chariot on your left?"

His languid motions and skimpy speech stirred a little smile on my lips, and I said, "From now on, Belacqua, I won't worry about you. But tell me, why are you sitting here? Are you expecting a guide? Or do you still have your old habits?"[9]

He said, "Brother, what good would it do me to climb up? God's winged angel sits at the gate, and he would not let me enter the disciplines ahead of time. First the heavens must revolve as many times while I wait here as they did during my life, because I breathed no repentant sighs until the end. Unless, of course, a prayer from a

---

[8] At that point in the journey Virgil (who represents human reason) will disappear and Beatrice (who represents divine love) will become Dante's guide. Human reason will have no more to say beyond that point.

[9] Dante is delighted to find that his old friend Belacqua is not in Hell and will eventually get to heaven. He had been a maker of musical instruments and notoriously lazy.

heart of grace rises up to help me. (What good are prayers that heaven wouldn't hear?)"

The poet was already climbing on ahead of me, saying, "Come on now; you see how the sun is touching the meridian here, and the foot of Night is already stepping on the ocean shore of Morocco."

PIA
Gustave Doré (Canto 5)

CANTO FIVE

Precious Shadow

I had just departed from these shades and was following in my guide's footsteps when behind me, pointing his finger, someone cried "Look! The sunlight does not fall to the ground on the left side of the second climber, and he seems to move like a live person."

At the sound of these words I turned and saw them all staring in astonishment at me—at me alone, and at the broken light.

"Why are you so easily distracted," my teacher said, "that you have paused? Why should you care what they whisper about? Follow me, and let people talk. Stand as firm as a tower that never sways when the winds are blasting. A man who lets one focus of attention compete with another doesn't get to his goal, because one preoccupation saps the strength of the other."

What could I answer except "I'm coming"? So I said it, a bit flushed with the color that sometimes shows that a person is contrite enough for pardon. Meanwhile, up the mountainside, some people crossed our path ahead singing Psalm 51 verse by verse.[1]

But when they saw that the sunlight didn't pass through my body, they let their song change into a

---

[1]This penitential psalm of David begins with the words "Have mercy on me, O God, according to your unfailing love; according to your great compassion blot out my transgressions. Wash away all my iniquity and cleanse me from my sin." In verse 17 David declares, "The sacrifices of God are a broken spirit; a broken and contrite heart, O God, you will not despise" (NIV). The spirits were singing this Psalm in Latin, and the opening phrase in Latin is "Miserere mei, Domine..."

prolonged gasp of "Ohhh!" Two of them served as messengers and ran to meet us, asking "Tell us about yourselves."

My teacher answered, "You may go back to those who sent you and tell them that the body of this man is mortal flesh. If it was his shadow that made them stop, as I suspect, that's what they want to know. If they are gracious to him, he may prove valuable to them."

I never saw a shooting star slice the clear sky at evening, or summer lightning slice the August clouds at sunset, so swiftly as they sped upward. When they arrived, they all wheeled around and headed down toward us like a cavalry troop turned loose.

"This is a large crowd coming," my teacher said, "and they all want favors from you. But keep on climbing, and listen while you climb."

"O soul, heading toward joy with the arms and legs you were born with," they cried, "wait a minute. See if you ever knew any of us before, so that you can report on us back home. Please, why are you hurrying so? Please, why won't you stop?

"We were all sinners up to our last hour, and all violently killed. Then the light of God enlightened us so that, repenting our sins and pardoning others for theirs, we left our earthly life reconciled to God, who now stabs us with desire to be with Him."

I said, "As hard as I am trying, I can't recognize any of you. But if there is anything I can do for you spirits who are born for bliss, tell me. I will do it for the sake of that peace which—in the footsteps of my guide—I am chasing from world to world."

One of them began, "Each of us trusts you to help us if you have the power to do so, without your having to promise. Therefore I, speaking first, pray that if you ever see the country which lies between Romagna and Naples, ask those in Fano to pray for me that I may be cleansed of my heavy sins. That was my home, but the deep wounds from which my life blood flowed away were dealt to me in the region of Padua. I was murdered where I thought I was safest. An Este who was unreasonably angry with me had it done. If I had fled towards La Mira, when I was set upon at Oriaco, I would still be over there where men breathe. But I fled to the marshes, and the reeds and mud entangled me so that I fell. And there I saw a pool spreading on the ground from my veins."[2]

Then another one said, "I pray of you — and may your desire drawing you up this high mountain be satisfied — with kind pity, help my desire. I am Buonconte, who was from Montrefeltro. My widow Giovanna and others neglect my memory, which is why I am so downcast."

I asked him, "What violence or twist of fate took you so far from Campaldino that no one ever found your burial place?"

"Oh," he answered, "at the foot of Casentino there is a stream named Archiano that flows down from the Apennines above the Hermitage. At the place where it merges into the Arno I arrived with my throat cut, flying on foot and bleeding all the way. There everything went black and my last word was the name of Mary; and there I fell, and my body was left alone.

"I'll tell you the truth and hope you tell it to the living. The angel of God took me, and the angel of Hell cried, 'You from Heaven, why do you steal my prey? You can take away the eternal part of this man, because one little tear he shed snatches him from me; but I get what's left of him.'"

"You know how the dampness goes up and then condenses in the cold. With his evil will that seeks only

---

[2]Jacobo del Cassero was an official at Bologna who thought it best to transfer to Milan because he knew that the nobleman Azzo VIII of Este resented him. But on his way to Milan, in 1298, he was murdered by Azzo's orders in a marshy area now called the dead lagoon.

harm, and with his intellect, he stirred the mist and wind according to his natural powers. That evening he covered the valley from Pratomagno to the mountains with mist and darkened the sky so that the saturated air turned to water. The rain poured, forming streams which united into great torrents, rushing swiftly to the great river. Then the raging Archiano found my body frozen in place where pain had overcome me. It uncrossed my arms from across my chest and swept me into the Arno and rolled me along its banks and over its bed, then covered me and wrapped me in debris."[3]

A third soul followed the second one. "Pray," she said, "when you return to the world and are rested from your long journey, remember me, La Pia. Sienna made me, and Maremma unmade me. This is well known to the one who was engaged to me, then wed me with the ring set with his gem."[4]

---

[3]Buonconte was killed in the battle of Campaldino on 11 June 1289, and his body was never found. (It is said that Dante took part in this battle on the other side.) This man's last-minute contrition, symbolized by one lonely tear, saved his soul. In contrast, all of Canto 27 in *The Inferno* tells the story of his father Guido of Montrefeltro, who became a Franciscan monk and a friend of the Pope in order to escape Hell and go to Heaven. But Guido trusted in absolution and did not experience the true contrition of Psalm 51. When Guido died, St. Francis came for his soul but a black cherubim came also, saying, "Don't take him! Don't cheat me!... Perhaps you did not realize that I was a logician!" Hell's angel was only able to sweep away Buonconte's body in a river, but it had been able to encase his father's soul in a writhing and flickering flame in Hell.

[4]The traditional identification of La Pia (Piety) is Pia dei Tolomei, who married Nello dei Pannocchieschi. In 1295 he took her to his castle in Maremma and killed her. Dante's Pia is noted for her modest brevity and her courtesy to Dante.

CANTO SIX

Away from the Eager Crowd

When a game of dice is over, the loser remains behind reviewing every toss that was made, feeling sadder but wiser. Everyone else goes away with the winner—one goes in front, one tugs at him from behind, and another is at his side so he won't be forgotten. The winner keeps on walking and listening to them; and when he slips them gifts, they quit crowding him so he can have some space. That's how I was in that crowd of spirits, acknowledging one here and one there, and making promises in order to get free from them.

There was the Aretine who met his death beneath the savage hand of Ghin di Tacco.[1] And one who drowned when he was fleeing from danger. There with his hands outstretched in prayer was Federigo Novello, and the man from Pisa who caused good Marzucco to show his moral strength.[2] I saw Count Orso.[3] Pier de la Brosse's soul was cut off from his body because of hatred and envy, he said, not for sinning. (Here let the Lady of Brabant take warning

---

[1] This was a judge who condemned a relative of Tacco, a notorious bandit. In vengeance, Tacco cut off the judge's head.

[2] Farinata of Pisa was the son of Marzucco; and when Farinata was killed by Count Ugolino, his good father opposed vengeance.

[3] Count Orso was killed in 1286 by his cousin Alberto. Their fathers had killed each other, and Dante had seen the fathers frozen together in Canto 33 of the *Inferno*.

while she is still on earth, so she won't end up in a worse crowd than he did.)[4]

Eventually I got free from all these souls whose one prayer was that others should pray for them so they could reach blessedness faster. Then I said, "My Light, it seems that you flatly denied in a certain passage of poetry that prayer can change Heaven's decree;[5] yet that is what these people pray for. Is their hope in vain? Or do I misunderstand your words?"

He answered me, "My words are plain enough, and yet their hope is not in vain if you put your whole mind to the problem. For the mountaintop of justice is not lowered an inch when the fire of love pays off instantly the debt that someone down here owes. In contrast, where I made my point the debt could not be paid off through prayer, because there prayer could not get through to God.[6]

"But in such a deep matter, don't settle until the woman explains it to you who will light the way between your mind and truth. I don't know if you understand; I'm speaking of Beatrice, and you will see her on this mountaintop, smiling and blessed."

I said, "My teacher, let's move faster. I'm not as tired as I was—and see, our side of the mountain is now in shadow."

"We will go as far as we can today," he answered, "but the truth is different from what you think. Before you get to the mountaintop, you will see the return of the

---

[4]Pier was one who accused Mary of Brabant of poisoning her son's half-brother in 1276 so her son would be next in line for the throne of France. Two years later Pier was hanged for treason, and Mary of Brabant had probably framed him with forged letters.

[5]Dante is referring to a passage in *Aeneid VI* where the soul of Palinurus is denied its request: "Cease to hope that the decrees of the gods are to be altered by prayers."

[6]The prayer that could not get through to God was spoken in Hell by a pagan.

sun, which is now hidden behind the mountain so that your body no longer breaks the sunbeams. But look ahead at that lone solitary soul gazing at us; it will tell us the quickest path to take."

We came to it. O soul from Lombardy, how proud and disdainful you seemed, and with what calm majesty you looked at us. It said nothing to us, but allowed us to approach, watching us like a lion at rest.

Nevertheless, Virgil drew close and asked it to show us the best way upward. The spirit did not answer his request, but asked us for our homeland and our identities. My sweet guide began to answer, "Mantua..." and the soul, which had been so withdrawn, leaped up from where it had been resting and said, "O man of Mantua, I am Sordello, from your city."[7] Then the two embraced each other.

Oh Italy—you slave, you heartbreak hotel, you pilotless ship in a storm! Not the lady of provinces, but of a brothel! Sordello's gentle soul was quick, at the mere mention of the sweet name of his city, to greet his fellow-citizen. Yet those who are alive within you now can't live together without warring, and those inside your wall and moat devour each other.

Miserable one, search around your seacoasts and inland and see if there is any part of you that enjoys peace. What use was it for Justinian to mend your bridle if your saddle was empty? It makes your shame worse.[8]

You, church leaders, should be obedient and let Caesar sit in the saddle, if you understood well what God

---

[7]Sordello was born about ten miles from Mantua in about 1200 and disappeared from history shortly after Dante's birth. He was the most outstanding Italian troubador poet, and the fact that he wrote political poetry causes Dante to do the same at this point.

[8]Justinian codified the Roman law circa 550 A.D., but there is no one to administer it anymore because there is no proper emperor.

directs.[9] See how this beast Italy has grown vicious because of not being guided by any spurs since you grabbed the bridle.

You, German Albert, neglecting her when she is running wild, instead of riding in the saddle—may punishment fall from the stars upon your family, something so bizarre and obvious that whoever follows you will be afraid. For you and your father, concentrating upon northern Europe because of your greed, have allowed the garden of the Roman Empire to be trampled down.[10]

Come, carefree Albert, and see the Montagues and Capulets.[11] See the Monaldi and Filipeschi, the grieving and the terrified.

Come, heartless ruler, come to see the ruin of your nobles and to tend their wounds, and to see how safe the region of Santafior is.[12]

Come and see Rome, weeping like a lonely widow day and night, crying "My dear Caesar, why aren't you with me?"[13]

Come and see how much your people love each other.[14] And if you have no pity for us, come because of the damage to your own reputation.

---

[9]Dante condemns the Church for usurping temporal power, and refers to the words of Jesus in Matthew 22:21, "Render therefore to Caesar the things which are Caesar's; and to God the things that are God's."

[10]Albert I of Austria became Emperor in 1298, but he ignored the domestic chaos in Italy and did not try to restore law and order there. Dante wished doom upon Albert in 1300 according to the story; but in fact when Dante wrote this Albert had already been assassinated by his nephew in 1308.

[11]In a little less than 300 years, Shakespeare would immortalize the tragic feud of the Montagues and Capulets in *Romeo and Juliet*.

[12]Santafior was full of robbers.

[13]The two Emperors in this period, Albert and his father Rudolph, never visited Italy once.

And if I am allowed to ask, highest Jove, You who came to earth to be crucified, are Your just eyes turned elsewhere? Or are You making secret preparation, in the depth of Your wisdom, for some good and holy outcome that we can't yet see? For the cities of Italy are all full of tyrants, and every clown that joins a faction becomes a new Marcellus.[15]

Now, Florence, you may be enjoying this digression that doesn't mention you so far, thanks to your people who function so well. Many people keep justice deep in their hearts and shoot it slowly and thoughtfully from the bow; but your people have it ready on the tip of the tongue. Many people refuse the burden of public office, but your people volunteer without being asked, and cry out, "I'll accept the job!"

Now rejoice, for you have cause: you are rich, you are at peace, you are wise. If that's true, the facts won't contradict it.

Athens and Sparta, which built codes of law and led the way in civilization, had only hinted at good living compared to you.[16] You plan so cleverly that thread you spin in October is unwound by mid-November. How often in recent memory you have changed your laws, coinage, offices, and customs; and even your members.

If you can recall yourself with clarity, you will see yourself like a sick woman who can find no rest upon her

---

[14]Dante is, of course, indulging in sarcasm.

[15]Dante asks God what grief-stricken people often ask: is God looking away, or is He preparing a remedy? According to Dorothy Sayers, Dante's mention of Marcellus refers to a Roman consul who opposed Julius Caesar and the Empire 1300 years earlier. He means that every demagogue who defies the constitution is now hailed as a hero.

[16]Dante ironically compares the productive stability of Athens and Sparta circa 500 B.C. to the destructive chaos of Florence in 1300 A.D.

feather bed, tossing and turning to try to escape her pain.[17]

---

[17]Dante laments the constant political tumult in Florence. Allen Mandelbaum points out how the tossing of the woman in pain at the end of Canto 6 slightly echoes the tossing of the dice and the pain of the gambler at the opening of Canto 6.

CANTO SEVEN

A Valley of Flowers

After the two had repeated their glad, gracious greeting three or four times, Sordello drew back and said "Who are you?"

"Before any spirits fit to ascend to God were ever brought to this mountain, my bones had already been buried by Octavian.[1] I am Virgil; and the only sin that lost Heaven for me was my lack of faith." That is how my guide answered.

Like one who suddenly sees something amazing, who believes and disbelieves, saying "It's true!—No, it can't be," so was Sordello. Then he bowed his head, returned to my guide, and sank to embrace his feet.

"O glory of the Latin race," he said, "by whom our language showed forth all its power, eternally praised where I was born, what could I ever do to deserve to see you here? If I am worthy to hear your words, tell me if you have come here from Hell, and from which section."

"Through all the circles of that woeful realm, I came here," he answered. "A power from Heaven propelled me, and that is how I came. It was not for what I did, but for what I failed to do, that I have lost sight of the high Sun whom you desire. I learned of Him too late.

---

[1]Virgil died under the reign of Octavian (Caesar Augustus) in 19 B.C., about fifty years before Christ had released the souls that were waiting in Limbo to move upward toward Heaven. According to traditional teaching in Dante's day, no human souls went to Purgatory or Heaven until Christ made that provision after His death and burial.

"Down below there is a place sad with darkness, not with pains—where the lamenting is not screams, but sighs. There I live with the innocent babies who were bitten by the fangs of death before they were freed from the sinful nature of the human race. There I live with those who failed to cover themselves with the three holiest virtues, although they knew and followed the other virtues without fail.[2]

"But if you know and are allowed to do so, show us how we can most quickly get to the real beginning of Purgatory."

He answered, "We are not limited to one spot; I'm allowed to climb and move about. So far as I'm allowed to go, I'll be your guide. But you see that the day is dwindling, and we cannot climb at night. Therefore it's best to locate a good resting place. There are some souls over to our right. If you agree, I will lead you to them; and you will be glad to meet them."[3]

"How is that?" he was answered. "If one wanted to climb at night, would people stop him, or would he simply find it impossible?"

Then the good Sordello drew a line ahead on the ground with his finger and said, "Look, you could not

---

[2]The virtuous souls in Limbo had four great traditional virtues: common sense, justice, courage, and self control. But they had not received the three great Christian virtues: faith, hope, and spiritual love.

[3]Dorothy Sayers points out that on earth these people were too much preoccupied with worldly cares rather than spiritual purpose. They are in a beautiful place because their concern was for others rather than themselves, but they are still preoccupied. In his story Dante usually sees the most illustrious people in each category. "But we need not doubt that he would place in this class not only kings and statesmen, but also humbler examples of the Preoccupied, such as anxious parents, over-burdened housewives and breadwinners, social workers, busy organizers, and others who are so 'rushed off their feet' that they forget to say their prayers."

even cross this line after sundown, for the simple reason that the darkness of night keeps us from stepping upward. It paralyzes our will to ascend. On the other hand, at night, while daylight is locked away behind the horizon, one can return downward or wander around at the same level."[4]

Then my master said, "Take us where you say we may enjoy our wait." We had gone ahead a short way when I saw a hollow in the mountainside just like a mountain valley at home.

"There," said the soul, "we will go where the mountainside provides a lap for us, and wait for the new day."

The winding path, sometimes steep, sometimes flat, led us to a low point on the valley's edge. Gold and fine silver, crimson cloth and bright white paint, rich highly-polished wood, freshly cracked emeralds — all these colors would look dull next to the grass and flowers in that valley, just as less is always overcome by more.

Besides her painting there, Nature had blended a thousand sweet scents into one, unfamiliar and indescribable.

There, seated on the grass and flowers, I saw souls who couldn't be seen from outside the valley. They were singing Salve Regina.[5]

The soul from Mantua who had led us there said, "Until the low sun sinks into his nest, don't ask me to take

---

[4]Dorothy Sayers explains that nights in Purgatory correspond to those times of spiritual darkness or dryness in life when the Sun (God) is not evident. The illumination of the grace of God is essential for progress toward God, and sometimes one must wait patiently for renewal of the light.

[5]This is the traditional evening hymn beginning "Hail, O Queen, Mother of mercy, our life, our sweetness and our hope, hail! To thee we cry, the exiled children of Eve, to thee we sigh, weeping and lamenting in this valley of tears."

you down among them.[6] From up here you can observe all
their movements and faces better than if you were with
them in the valley.

"He who sits highest and looks as if he left undone
something he should have done, and who does not move
his lips with the others' singing, was the Emperor Rudolph
who could have healed the wounds that destroyed Italy.
Too late, another may try to help her.

"The one trying to comfort him ruled the land where
the water begins that runs down the Moldau into the Elbe,
and down the Elbe into the sea. He was named Ottocar,
and in diapers he was a better man than his bearded son
Wenceslas, consumed with lust and laziness.[7]

"And the snub-nosed one, leaning close to talk to the
one with a kind face, died in flight, dishonoring the lily.
See how he beats his breast. The other, who is sighing, has
made a bed for his cheek in the palm of his hand. They are
father and father-in-law of the plague of France. They
know his filthy and foul life, the source of the grief that
cuts them so.[8]

---

[6]Geoffrey Nuttall points out on p. 51 of *The Faith of Dante Alighieri*.
"Without often mentioning children, Dante sees to it that throughout
Purgatorio what is little is never long out of our minds. The sun is the
little sun, *il poco sole*, now sinking to its nest. The Valley of the Rulers is
a little valley, *la picciola vallea*." In Canto 28 the brook will have little
waves and Matilda will take a ballerina's tiny steps. Birds, flowers,
trees, grass, and leaves are all young and tender. *Purgatory* has more
than twice as many diminutives as the other two books of the *Comedy*
combined.

[7]It is significant that King Ottocar of Bohemia is comforting
Emperor Rudolph in Purgatory because in 1278 Rudolph killed Ottocar
in battle. (In Hell no earthly enemies were reconciled.)

[8]The snub-nosed man is Philip III of France. He had disgraced the
lily, still the symbol of France today, with his cowardly defeat in battle
in 1285. He is with kind-faced King Henry I of Navarre. They are
grieving about Philip IV, the plague of France, whom Dante scorned.

"The muscular one, who sings in harmony with the one with the hook-nose, wore a belt of every merit. And if the younger one who sits behind him had become king after him, family merit might have poured from one vessel to the next, which may not be said of the other heirs. James and Frederick inherited his realms, but no one inherited his fine qualities.[9] Human excellence rarely keeps rising through family branches; and this is the will of the one who gives excellence, so that one may pray to Him for it.

"Those words also apply to the one with the big nose, no less than to Peter who sings with him, the reason Apulia and Provence are moaning. The plant is worth less than the seed it came from, just as Constance had more to boast about in her husband than Beatrice and Margaret did in theirs.[10]

"Look at the King Henry of England, who led a simple life, seated there alone. His branches bore better offspring.[11]

"That one sitting below the others looking up at them is William the Marquis, who caused the rebellious city of

---

[9] The muscular king is Peter (Pedro) III of Aragon, who married Manfred's daughter Constance. (At the end of Canto 3, Manfred asked Dante to ask his daughter Constance to pray for him.) Peter is singing in harmony with Charles of Anjou, who was his bitter enemy on earth. The young man with Peter is probably his beloved son Peter, who died very young.

[10] Dante is saying that families often go downhill. Apulia and Provence are suffering under the inferior sons of Peter III. Charles II and his brother Louis IX (husbands of Beatrice and Margaret) were inferior to their father Charles of Anjou (with the large nose); and Charles II was also inferior to Peter III.

[11] Henry III was a rather incompetent and neglectful king noted for his great piety. Dorothy Sayers speculates that he is at this level of Purgatory because "to pray when one ought to be working is as much a sin as to work when one ought to be praying."

Alessandria to bring grief to his cities of Montferrato and Canvese."[12]

---

[12]William VII tried to put down a rebellion in the city of Alessandria, and leaders there locked him in an iron cage for exposure to public ridicule for seventeen months, until his death in 1292. When his son tried to avenge his father, men from Allesandria invaded Montferrato and Canvese and brought more grief.

CANTO EIGHT

Green-winged Angels

It was the hour that turns the desire of seafarers toward home and melts their hearts, at the end of the day when they have told their dear friends goodbye. It was the hour when a new traveler feels a pang in his heart if he hears chimes that seem to mourn the dying day.[1] That is when I stopped listening to Sordello and gave my attention to a spirit who rose up and signaled for us to be quiet.[2]

He joined his palms and raised his hands with his eyes fixed on the east, as if to say to God "I care for nothing except you."[3]

The hymn "To thee before the light is gone" poured so sweetly from his mouth, with such sweet music, that I forgot myself entirely. And the others sweetly and devoutly accompanied him through the entire hymn, with their eyes fixed on the stars.[4]

---

[1] These nostalgic lines about homesickness are so popular that they have been translated dozens of times. But the homesickness that strikes these souls in the valley is the homesickness for heaven.

[2] At the end of Canto 7 Dante was absorbed in Sordello's references to the disappointing, disillusioning, and disastrous worldly careers of several well-known souls. Now there is a great shift of attention, and that is the whole point of Purgatory.

[3] These souls are learning to give their attention to God.

[4] The hymn the souls sang in Latin is "*Te lucis ante*" (Before the ending of the day), a prayer of St. Ambrose that asks God for protection from evil dreams and night hauntings. When Dante and Virgil were

Readers, now look sharply for the truth; for the veil of allegory is very thin, and it should be easy to see my meaning.

I saw that company of noblemen silently gazing upward in expectation, pale and humble. Then I saw two angels appear on high and come on down, with flaming swords that were broken off, without any points.[5]

Their garments were as green as tender, newly opened leaves, billowing behind them and rippled by their green wings. One came and alighted a bit above us and the other alighted on the opposite bank, so that the souls were safely between them. I could clearly see their radiant hair, but my eyes were dazzled by their faces — as if stunned by more than human senses can take in.

"Both angels come from Mary," Sordello said, "to guard the valley from a serpent that will soon appear." Not knowing where it would come from, at that point I turned icy cold and huddled close to the trusty shoulders. Then Sordello added, "Now we'll descend into the valley to speak to the great souls there. They will rejoice to see you."

It seemed like only three steps down to the valley floor, and there I saw a soul gazing at me as if he recognized my face. It was the time when the air was darkening, but not yet so dark that we could not see each other clearly. He stepped toward me, and I stepped toward him. Noble

---

entranced with Casella's love song in Canto 2, they were distracted from their purpose. This time Dante's transport was correct.

[5]The flaming swords of the two angels remind readers of the two angels guarding the Garden of Eden in Genesis 3:24. The fact that the swords have no points anymore may mean that the victory against evil has already been won and in this place the swords are symbolic. The green of the great angel wings and fluttering garments is a sign of hope for salvation. This valley is like an imperfect foretaste of the transcendent Garden of Eden awaiting the travelers at the top of Mount Purgatory.

Judge Nino! How I rejoiced when I saw that you were here and not damned![6]

No words of welcome were left unsaid between us. Then he asked, "How long is it since you came to the foot of this mountain from across the far sea?"

"Oh," I answered, "I came this morning from the realms of misery, and I'm still in my first life—although by this journey I'll earn the other life."

When they heard this answer, he and Sordello shrank back in shock. One of them turned to Virgil, and the other turned to a soul seated nearby and cried, "Get up, Conrad! Come to see what the grace of God has willed!"

Then he turned to me and said, "By all the special gratitude that you owe to Him who hides His reason so deep that no one can wade out to it, I ask you—when you get back beyond the wide waters, tell my little Giovanna to pray for me there where pure prayers are heard. I do not think her mother loves me anymore, since she set aside her widow's headcovering which she will soon wish she had back again. By her example it is easy to see how long the fire of love lasts in a woman when looks and touches are no longer there to fan the flame.[7] The serpent from her

---

[6]Nino Visconte was a grandson of Count Ugolino, whose horrible ending was described in *The Inferno*, Canto 33. He was also the judge who had his deputy hanged for accepting bribes to let prisoners escape, as described in *The Inferno*, Canto 22. Dante is genuinely delighted to see his friend Nino safely on his way to heaven in spite of the fact that on earth he had not been devoted to God. Dorothy Sayers comments about Nino, "What qualifies a soul for Purgatory is not innocence, but repentance."

[7]Nino hopes that his daughter Giovanni will pray for him. He resents the fact that in 1300, four years after his death, his widow married another nobleman. He thinks she will regret her remarriage because in 1302 the fortunes of her new husband will go bad. One can only wonder if Nino's bitter words about his widow's lack of love for him expressed Dante's own feeling about his wife Gemma back in Florence.

new husband's shield in Milan will not make such a fine
emblem on her future tomb as the cock from my shield
would have done."[8] While he spoke this way, his face was
stamped with a look of restrained anger burning in the
heart.

My hungry eyes were turned back toward the part of
the sky where the stars are slowest, like the part of a wheel
closest to the axle.[9] My guide said, "Son, what are you
gazing at up there?"

I said to him, "At those three lights which flame near
the south polar region."

He said, "The four bright stars you saw this morning
are out of sight, and these have risen where they were."[10]

As he was speaking, Sordello pulled him close and
said, "See there—our enemy!" and pointed his finger
where Virgil should look.

And where the little valley had no bank of protection,
there was a snake, perhaps like the one that gave Eve such
bitter fruit. Through the grass and flowers the evil streak
slid, turning its head now and then to lick its back, like a
beast that sleeks itself.[11]

---

[8]Nino's family was older and more aristocratic than that of his
widow's new husband. In Dante's time the family insignia was carved
on the wife's tomb.

[9]The stars closest to the poles seem to be slowest because their
circles are smallest.

[10]Half the stars in the night sky are hidden from Dante because he is
low on the east side of an extremely high mountain. The point here is
that the four virtues common to all good people are now replaced by the
three distinctly Christian virtues: faith, hope, and spiritual love.

[11]In her essay "...And Telling You a Story" Dorothy Sayers remarks
about the loveliness of *Purgatory* to this point: "the dew-drenched grass
and swaying reeds, the faint shimmering of the sea, the boat, seen
through the mist like Mars rising, and gradually revealing the white
wings of the heavenly pilot, the eager souls singing as they come and
gladly leaping to the shore—the whole picture is of a translucent and
tender and unearthly beauty so utterly unlike anything in the *Inferno*

I didn't see and cannot tell how the heavenly falcons moved, but I clearly saw them both in flight. Hearing the green wings slice the air, the serpent fled; and the angels wheeled around, flying like twins back to their posts.[12]

The soul that had come to the judge when summoned had not taken his eyes off me once during that attack. He said now, "So may the guiding light that leads to what you seek find in your will as much lamp-oil as is needed for you to reach the brightly colored mountaintop.[13] If you know accurate news of Valdimacra or that neighborhood, tell me—because I was once mighty there. I was called Conrad Malaspina; not the original, but descended from him. For my family I had love that has to be purified here."[14]

"Oh," I answered, "I have never been through your land, but everyone who lives in Europe knows about it. The fame that honors your house recommends its owners

---

that the sense of relief and escape is almost physical. Equally lovely, though touched in with slightly stronger tints, is the Valley of the Rulers, with its enameled flowers, green-robed angels, and the sliding glitter of the snake. The landscape, as well as the poetry and the 'feel' of the first eight cantos of the *Purgatorio*, is of a quality so rare and strange that criticism has invented no suitable language to describe it."

[12]Dorothy Sayers says that the souls in this place below Purgatory are still liable to temptation and sin in the subconscious, the region of dreams, which is not yet subject to the will. For Christians on earth, "The episode may perhaps be taken to mean that so long as the will *truly* intends penitence and amendment, the Christian need not, and should not, be unduly troubled about the involuntary aberrations of the unconscious, but should simply commend the matter to God, in the confident assurance that it will be taken care of."

[13]Conrad refers to Christ's parable (recorded in Matthew 25:1-13) of five wise virgins who provided extra oil for their lamps and five foolish virgins who ran out of lamp-oil. Those without adequate oil were too late for the wedding banquet (the mountaintop).

[14]Conrad evidently concentrated on his fine family to the neglect of God, which is why he finds himself down among the Preoccupied in Purgatory.

and its countryside to people who have never been there. I promise you, and I would stake the rest of my journey on this, that your honored clan has not lost first place in wealth and self defense. Environment and heredity so bless your family that although the guilty head sets all the world awry, your people alone walk straight and shun the path of evil."[15]

Conrad answered, "There you go. For the sun won't rest seven times in its sky bed beneath the four feet of the Ram constellation before this gracious opinion will be nailed into your head with stronger nails than mere hearsay can provide—if what has been ordained comes to pass."[16]

---

[15]The "guilty head that sets the world awry" is obviously Satan, although Dante might have been referring also to the evil Pope Boniface VIII.

[16]Conrad rightly predicts that before seven years have passed, Dante will in 1306 take refuge with a branch of the generous Malaspina family and know for himself their excellence. In 1300, when this prophecy is spoken, Dante has not yet been exiled. In 1312 or thereabouts, when Dante wrote this canto, he was looking back upon the great kindness of the Malaspinas to him and expressing his gratitude.

CANTO NINE

Peter's Gate

Now upon her eastern balcony the bedmate of ancient Tithonus grew white after leaving the arms of her sweet lover. Her forehead was glittering with gems, set in the design of a small cold-blooded beast that strikes people with its tail.[1]

And Night, where we were, had gone up two of the steps she must climb, and was winging up the third, when I—still a human son of Adam—was overwhelmed with sleepiness and stretched out on the grass where all five of us were sitting.[2]

At the hour when the swallow begins her sad morning song (perhaps in memory of long-ago sorrow), and when our mind wanders farther from the body and is less held

---

[1] In Greek mythology Tithonus was a warrior married to Aurora (sunrise), but he was cursed with eternal life without protection from aging. Scholars disagree about whether Dante meant sunrise or moonrise here. The moon was in the constellation of the Scorpion on this date, and those stars were like gems. (Scorpions with tails that sting are mentioned in Revelation 9:10.)

[2] Dante probably means that two hours and most of the third have passed since sunset, and it is almost 9 p.m. This is the first time he has gone to sleep on his journey, and he will continue to need occasional sleep as long as he is in Purgatory. He never needed sleep in Hell, and he will never need sleep in Heaven, because both of those places are in eternity. But Purgatory is a temporary place in time, and as a living human he needs his sleep there. His four companions on the grass are Virgil, Sordello, Judge Nino, and Conrad.

back by ordinary thought, our dreams become somewhat prophetic.[3]

In my dream I thought I saw an eagle poised in the sky with golden pinions, ready to swoop. It seemed as if I were at the very spot where Gannymede left his friends behind, carried away to the high gods.[4] I thought to myself, "Perhaps because of habit he hunts in this spot only, and perhaps he refuses to carry up prey from anywhere else." Then it seemed to me that after wheeling awhile, terrible as lightning, he plunged and snatched me up as high as the circle of fire.[5] There we burned together, and the flame was so hot that it woke me up.

It was like this when Achilles woke up, casting his eyes about and wondering where he was, when his mother carried his sleeping form away from his tutor Chiron to the Isle of Scyros, from which later the Greeks lured him away. So I jerked up, as soon as sleep left my eyes, and went pale like a man frozen with terror. The only person by me was my comforter, and the sun was over two hours high; I was looking out toward the sea.[6]

---

[3]Observant dreamers have always noticed that dreams near the end of the daily sleep cycle are unusual; and in the second half of the twentieth century, brain-monitoring technology has verified this fact. During his time in Purgatory, Dante tells of three such dreams.

[4]Gannymede, beautiful son of the mythological founder of Troy, was carried off to Olympus by an eagle. To Dante the Trojans were special chosen people because they became the founders of Rome, and Rome became the center of Christianity.

[5]According to tradition, an old eagle would fly up high into the circle of fire, then fall into a fountain of water where he was reborn as a young eagle. This story was a symbol of baptism.

[6]Because the sun rose at 6 a.m. this Monday morning on the day after Easter in the year 1300, we know that Dante did not awaken until a bit after 8 a.m. He had slept over eleven hours and had been moved far uphill in his sleep without awakening. Dorothy Sayers says that Dante is now at about the level of the highest peak of Mt. Everest, which is about five and a half miles above sea level.

"Don't be afraid," my master said. "You are safe, because we are in a good place. Don't shrink back, but summon all your strength. You have now arrived at Purgatory proper.[7] Look at the embankment that surrounds it, and see the opening up there.

"Earlier, in the dawn before daybreak, when your soul slept inside your body upon the flowers adorning the ground, a lady came to us. She said, 'I am Lucy. Let me pick up this sleeping man to help him on his way.'

"Sordello and the noblemen stayed behind. She carried you upward in the morning light, and I followed in her footsteps. She laid you here after her lovely eyes showed me that open entrance; then she and your sleep disappeared together."

Just as a frightened man can be reassured, and his fear turns to comfort once he learns the truth, so I changed. When my leader saw that I was free from alarm, he started up the rampart, with me following, toward the height.

Reader, you can see how I lift up my subject for you. Don't be surprised if I have to use even greater skill to keep holding it up.

We drew near and arrived at the place where I had seen the opening just like a crack that splits a wall. I spied a gate with three steps of different hues leading up to it, with a guard who hadn't said a word. As I stared, I saw that he was seated on the top step, and his face was such that I could not look at it. In his hands he held a naked sword that reflected such light toward us that I tried to look at it in vain.

---

[7]This is the beginning of the main section of *Purgatory*.

"Stop there and tell me what you want," he began. "Who comes to escort you? Be careful about coming up, so you won't get hurt!"[8]

My teacher answered him, "A heavenly lady who knows all about these things just now told us, 'Go over there to the gate.'"[9]

"May she speed you to your goodness," the kind guardian of the gate replied. "So come forward to our stairs."

There we came, and the first step was white marble so smooth and polished that I could see my reflection in it.[10]

The second step was darker than bluish-black, of rough and scorched stone, crossed with two great cracks.[11]

The third and highest step, which was massive, seemed to be of porphyry stone that flamed as red as any blood that spurts from a vein.[12]

On this upper step God's angel had both his feet, for he was sitting on the threshold, which seemed to me to be made of adamantine stone.[13]

---

[8]It is obvious that when waiting souls come up from the lower part of Mount Purgatory to enter, they must be brought by a heavenly messenger.

[9]Virgil had learned from the silver-haired guard at the foot of Mount Purgatory that a long flattering speech was not wanted in this realm, just heavenly credentials. He takes the liberty of translating Lucy's gesture into words.

[10]The first part of penitence is confession. The penitent person sees himself as he is, a sinner, and honestly confesses.

[11]The second part of penitence is contrition (grief for sin). Psalm 51:17 says "A broken and contrite heart, O God, thou shalt not despise."

[12]The third part of penitence is restitution. This includes an appropriation of Christ's sacrifice for the sins of the world, and a pouring out of one's own life and love.

[13]According to Dorothy Sayers, "The Threshold of adamant is the foundation on which the Church is built; in her human aspect, the Rock which is Peter; in her Divine aspect, the Cornerstone which is Christ."

Up these three steps my leader brought me with great
good will, and advised me, "Ask humbly for the lock to
be opened."

I flung myself devoutly at the guard's holy feet and
begged him to open it in his mercy. But first I struck my
chest three times.[14]

With the point of his sword he made seven P's on my
forehead and said, "Wash these wounds away when you
are inside."[15]

His garment was exactly the color of dust and ashes,
and from beneath it he drew out two keys. One was gold
and the other was silver. First with the white and then the
yellow key he worked the lock to satisfy me.[16]

"Whenever one of these keys fails to turn just right in
the lock," he told us, "the entrance won't open. One of
them is more precious, but the other requires great skill
and knowledge for it to work, because it is the one that
unties the knot. I got these from Peter, and he told me to
err on the side of opening the gate, rather than keeping it
shut, for anyone who falls at my feet."[17]

---

[14]When a Penitent makes confession to a priest he taps his chest three
times, indicating that he has sinned in thought, word, and deed. Dante
and his readers all took this knowledge for granted.

[15]P stands for the Latin word *peccatum*, which means sin. There are
traditionally seven major sins, and those are the ones that will be
washed away in Purgatory. Readers should remember that Dante aims
at changing people in this life.

[16]The golden key represents God's forgiveness for sin, bought on the
cross. The silver key represents removal of sin from the human heart.
The golden key alone results in "cheap grace" (which did not save
Guido in the *Inferno*, Canto 27), and the silver key alone results in
despair.

[17]This entire canto seems to echo James 4:8-10, "Come near to God
and he will come near to you. Wash your hands, you sinners, and purify
your hearts, you double-minded. Grieve, mourn, and wail. Change your
laughter to mourning and your joy to gloom. Humble yourselves before
the Lord, and he will lift you up" (NIV).

Then he pushed open the holy gate, saying "Enter, but I'm warning you that anyone who looks back finds himself outside again." When the pivots of that holy gate, made of resonant forged metal, began to turn in their sockets, they cried louder than Mount Tarpeia roared when the good guard Metellus was removed and she was made poor.[18]

Then he pushed open the holy gate, saying "Enter, but I'm warning you that anyone who looks back finds himself outside again." When the pivots of that holy gate, made of resonant forged metal, began to turn in their sockets, they cried louder than Mount Tarpeia roared when the good guard Metellus was removed and she was made poor.[19]

I spun toward the sound because I seemed to hear, in words mingled with sweet music, the hymn "We praise thee, O God."[20] What I heard gave the very same impression as when we hear people singing with an organ, when now the words are clear, and then they are not.

---

[18]Dante refers to the noisy opening of the great gates of the treasury of Rome on Mount Tarpeia after Caesar crossed the Rubicon. The guard Metellus tried to protect the city treasure, in vain. According to Dorothy Sayers, the pivots of Peter's Gate are rusty because so few men take the way of salvation. She quotes Matthew 7:14, "Strait is the gate and narrow is the way that leadeth unto life, and few there be that find it."

[19]Dante refers to the noisy opening of the great gates of the treasury of Rome on Mount Tarpeia after Caesar crossed the Rubicon. The guard Metellus tried to protect the city treasure, in vain. According to Dorothy Sayers, the pivots of Peter's Gate are rusty because so few men take the way of salvation. She quotes Matthew 7:14, "Strait is the gate and narrow is the way that leadeth unto life, and few there be that find it."

[20]In Latin the hymn by Saint Ambrose is *"Te Deum laudamus."* The sound of this hymn in *Purgatory* bears witness to Christ's words in Luke 15:10: "In the same way, I tell you, there is rejoicing in the presence of the angels of God over one sinner who repents."

CANTO TEN

Above the Needle's Eye

When we had crossed the threshold of that gate—
which is seldom used, because of the soul's evil loves that
make the crooked way seem straight—I heard it clang
shut. And if I had turned to look back, how could I have
found an adequate excuse?[1]

We climbed up through a split in the rock which
zigzagged like a sea wave that washes in and out.

"Here we must be extra careful," my leader began,
"inching up one side and then the other as they veer back
and forth."[2] This made our steps so small and slow that
the waning moon reached its bed and sank down to rest
before we emerged from that needle's eye.[3] So when we
came out free into the open air above, where the
mountainside is set back a bit, I was exhausted. We were

---

[1]The gatekeeper had sternly warned Dante not to look back. Dante
is now beginning his climb up the seven-story mountain, which lasts
from Canto 10 through Canto 27. On most of the seven ledges Dante
will encounter a penance, a meditation, a prayer, an angel, and a
benediction.

[2]The incline is steeper than 45 degrees, which explains the strenuous
maneuvering. The climbers had to switch from one side of the crack to
the other every time it zigzagged diagonally upward.

[3]This passageway reminds readers of Christ's words in Matthew
19:24: "Again I tell you, it is easier for a camel to go through the eye of a
needle than for a rich man to enter the kingdom of God." This is in
great contrast to the broad, easy entry to Hell. It was after 9:30 a.m.
when Dante and Virgil finally climbed out of the needle's eye.

both uncertain of our way, and we stood stock still on a flat ledge lonelier than a desert trail.[4]

From the ledge's outer edge where it dropped off into empty space, to the base of a sheer bank which climbs and climbs, a human body could stretch full-length three times; and so far as my eyes could fly in either direction, this was true.[5] Our feet had not yet moved at all when I realized that the inner bank, which was steep and impossible to climb, was of pure white marble and carved with sculptures that would put not only Polycletus, but nature herself, to shame.[6]

The angel that came to earth to announce the peace that had long been wept for, which opened heaven after its long restriction, appeared before us—his gracious form so vividly carved there that it didn't seem like a silent image.[7] One would have sworn that he was saying "Greetings," for there also was the one who turned the key that released supreme love.[8] And in her gestures one saw the phrase "I am the Lord's servant" as clearly as a seal imprints wax.

---

[4]This is the first and lowest of seven ledges that ring Mount Purgatory.

[5]The ledge was, at most, eighteen feet wide, with no railing of any kind and a five or six mile drop-off.

[6]The Greek sculptor Polycletus (circa 452-412 BC) was praised in Italy in Dante's day. In *The Inferno*, Canto 11, Virgil had explained that nature reflects the mind of God, and human art reflects nature. These scenes are directly from the mind of God.

[7]This is the angel Gabriel who came to Mary (as recounted in Luke 1, NIV) and announced that God had chosen her to bear the Messiah. Gabriel began by saying "Greetings, you who are highly favored! The Lord is with you." Her response ended in perfect humility: "I am the Lord's servant. May it be to me as you have said."

[8]Revelation 3:7 (NIV) refers to Christ: "These are the words of him who is holy and true, who holds the keys of David. What he opens no one can shut, and what he shuts no one can open." As Christ's mother, Mary in a sense "turned the key."

"Don't limit yourself to one scene," said my sweet teacher, who had me on his side where people have their hearts. So I turned my head and saw beyond Mary where my teacher was urging me to look—another story in the stone. I stepped past Virgil and drew close to it to see it clearly.

There was carved into the marble the oxcart carrying the Ark of the Covenant, which warns us not to take on tasks not meant for us.[9] In front, there were people divided into seven choirs; my ears said "no," but my eyes said "Yes, they sing!" In the same way, the smoke of the incense rising there made my eyes say yes and my nose say no.

Ahead of the Ark the humble Psalmist was dancing with his royal robes off, both more and less than a king at that moment. Watching from the window of a great palace was Michal, looking sad and scornful.[10]

My feet moved on from where I stood so I could peer closely at another story which glowed white beyond the figure of Michal. There the glory of a Roman prince was portrayed, whose excellence inspired Gregory on to victory. I mean the Emperor Trajan.[11]

---

[9] Dante refers to the fate of Uzzah, a servant of King David in about 1000 BC, who grabbed the Ark to steady it and was struck dead. (Some think that Uzzah's impetuous act was the result of pride.) Three months later King David brought the Ark the rest of the way into Jerusalem with much celebration, as recounted in 2 Samuel 6.

[10] David's proud wife Michal was embarrassed by his undignified display of joy and praise for God, and she scolded him afterwards. He answered "I will celebrate before the Lord. I will become even more undignified than this, and I will be humiliated in my own eyes" (2 Samuel 6:21-22, NIV).

[11] According to legend, St. Gregory (pope from 590 to 604 A.D.) so admired the compassionate humility of Trajan (emperor from 98 to 117 AD) that he prayed for Trajan's miraculous salvation and the prayer was granted.

A poor widow was clinging to his bridle, weeping with grief. Around him surged a crowd of horsemen, and golden eagles were waving above him in the wind. In the midst of all this, the poor creature seemed to say, "Lord, avenge me for the murder of my son, which has broken my heart."

He answered her, "Just wait until I return."

Like a person whose grief is urgent, she said, "Lord, what if you don't return?"

He answered, "The one who takes my place will do it for you."

She said, "Can the good deed of another substitute for one you neglected?"

He said, "All right, take heart. I see I have to fulfill my duty before I go. Justice requires it, and pity keeps me here."

He to whom nothing is ever new thus made conversation visible—something new to us because it is not seen on earth. I was rejoicing to see these pictures of great humility, all the more precious because of their Craftsman.

The poet murmured, "Look at the crowd coming with slow steps. They will direct us to the upward stairs." My eyes, which are always eager to see something new, turned toward him quickly.

Reader, I would not want you to be dismayed and lose heart through hearing how God chooses to have this debt paid. Pay no attention to the form of pain; think of what follows, and remember that the pain can't last beyond Judgment Day.

I said, "Teacher, what I see moving toward us doesn't look like people, but I can't tell what it is. My sight is confused."

He answered, "Their painful kind of torment doubles them down to the ground, so at first my eyes couldn't interpret. But look hard there and untangle with your eyes what is coming beneath those slabs of stone; you can see now how each one beats his breast."

O you proud Christians, wretched and weary, whose minds are sick, who put trust in backward steps, can't you tell that we are worms, born to be transformed into the angelic butterfly that flies to judgment with no self defense? Why do you expect to soar when you are still the unfinished grub, the worm that is waiting for a new shape?[12]

Just as one sometimes sees a bracket designed like a human with his knees to his chest bracing a roof or ceiling-beam, and this fantasy figure creates actual discomfort in the viewer—so it was when I looked hard at these souls.

True enough, they were bent down lower or not as low according to the amount of weight on their backs; but even the most patient-looking of them seemed to say with tears, "I can bear no more."

---

[12]The butterfly represents the perfected human soul. Pride is the first and worst of the seven deadly sins. Just as Dante's descent in Hell took him down in the darkness from the least evil to the most evil categories of sin, so Dante's ascent in Purgatory will take him up in sunlight from the most evil to the least evil sins.

The Portals of Purgatory
Gustave Doré (Canto 9)

CANTO ELEVEN

Prayer of the Proud

"Our Father, who is in heaven—not because of any limitation, but because of your great love for that part of your creation—may your name and worth be praised by every creature, because it is fitting to offer thanks for your sweet pouring forth of yourself.[1]

"May the peace of your kingdom come to us, for we cannot achieve it on our own with all our cleverness.

"Just as your angels offer up their wills to you, singing 'Hosannah,' may multitudes of humans do so also.

"Give us this day our daily manna, for without it even the one who struggles hardest to hurry through this harsh wilderness will only move backwards.

"And as we forgive all who have harmed us, may you kindly forgive us and disregard our record.

"Don't pit our strength, which is easily overcome, against the ancient foe; but deliver us from him who attacks. (This last prayer is not for ourselves, dear Lord, because we don't need it now. It is for those who remain behind us.)"[2]

Thus those souls, praying for progress for themselves and for us, moved along beneath their burdens as we

---

[1] The proud souls bent down under heavy slabs of stone are praying in unison an adaptation of the Lord's Prayer (Matthew 6:9-13 and Luke 11:2-4) which expresses the humility they are learning.

[2] Satan is no longer attacking the souls in Purgatory, and so they pray the ending of the Lord's Prayer for those they left behind.

sometimes move in dreams.[3] Each suffered his own degree of anguish, but all were fatigued and struggling along the ledge around the mountain, wearing away the world's foul scum.

If they say a good word for us there, what can be said and done for them here by people of good will? Surely we ought to help them wash away the stains they took there from this world, so that pure and light they can go on to starry spheres.

"Say there! I hope justice and pity soon unburden you, so that you may spread wings to lift you up where you want to go. Please show us whether to go right or left to get to the stairway as fast as possible. Or if there is more than one, show us the least steep—because my companion, weighed down by the flesh of Adam that he is wearing, is a slow climber in spite of his eagerness."[4]

It was not clear who spoke the words that answered these from the one I was following, but the voice said, "Come to the right, along the bank with us, and you shall find the stairway that a live person can climb. And if I were not impeded by the stone which bows my proud neck and forces me to carry my face so low, I would look at the one who is alive but hasn't identified himself, to see if I know him and to move him to pity for my burden.

"I was Italian and the son of a great man from Tuscany; Guglielmo Aldobrandesco was my father. I don't know if you ever heard of him.[5] The noble blood and

---

[3]During rapid-eye-movement dreams the body is actually semi-paralyzed, and the dreamer sometimes experiences a nightmarish inability to move except in slow motion.

[4]There is some unintentional irony in Virgil's mentioning the weight of Dante's flesh to souls who are weighed down by huge slabs of stone.

[5]Everyone in Italy would have heard of Omberto's famous father, and so when Omberto said that perhaps Dante hadn't heard of his father he was expressing great modesty.

gallant deeds of my ancestors made me so arrogant that I forgot our common mother and held everyone in such great scorn that it caused my death, as the Sienese know and every child knows in Campagnatico.[6]

"I am Omberto, and my pride did not harm me alone, for it was the ruin of all my family. And here I bear this load among the dead until God is satisfied, because I did not do it among the living."

I had bowed my face down close to listen, and another one of them, not the speaker, twisted himself beneath the load that weighed him down, and saw me and knew me and called to me while keeping his eyes on me with great difficulty—as I was moving along with them, bent down low.[7]

"Oh my," I said to him, "aren't you Oderisi, glory of the town of Gubbio and of the school of painting that in Paris is called illumination?"

"Brother," he answered, "the pages painted by Franco Bolognese are more delightful. The glory is all his, and only partly mine. I would not have been this courteous when I lived, because my heart was driven by such a strong desire to be the best. For that pride I am now paying the price; and I would not be here yet except that when I could still sin, I turned to God instead.

"What empty glory in human powers! How brief the period when praise stays green, unless the next generation is untalented! Cimabue thought he would stay first in

---

[6]Omberto forgot that he was descended from Eve, like everyone else, and that pride caused the fall of Adam and Eve. He was killed by the Sienese in 1259 at Campagnatico; his relatives perished, and the Sienese took their property.

[7]John Ciardi points out that Dante not only bowed down physically to hear Omberto, but he also bowed down spiritually in order to identify with those who are purifying themselves of pride.

painting; but now Giotto gets the praise, so the former's fame is eclipsed.[8]

"Likewise, one writer named Guido has taken from the other the glory of our language. And perhaps someone else is already born who will chase both songbirds from their nest.[9]

"Earthly fame is nothing but a breath of wind, which comes here and goes there, and changes name when it changes direction. What greater fame will you have in a thousand years if you strip off your flesh when you are old than if you had died before you had got beyond 'din-din' and 'penny'?[10] A thousand years is less in comparison to eternity than the blink of an eye in comparison to the turning of the slowest sphere.

"All Tuscany rang with the name of the man who moves along so slowly ahead of me, and now there is hardly a whisper of him in Siena. He ruled there when they defeated furious Florence—who was then a socialite, as she is now a prostitute.

"Glory is like the green of the grass, which comes and goes; the sun that caused it to spring up green from the ground also turns it brown."[11]

---

[8]Cimabue of Florence (circa 1240-1302) discovered Giotto (1266-1336) sketching a lamb on a stone while tending his father's sheep, and took him in as an art student. Cimabue's art is still admired at the end of the twentieth century, but Giotto's is considered far greater. It is believed that Giotto and Dante were personal friends, and the most popular portrait of Dante is commonly attributed to Giotto.

[9]The two writers named Guido were probably Guido Guinicelli and Dante's dear friend Guido Cavalcante who died in 1300. Many readers suspect that the "someone else" who may out-sing them is Dante's playful hint about himself.

[10]Oderisi claims that a lifetime of literary success won't mean any more glory in the long run than a few months of babytalk about food and money (two of adult life's main concerns).

[11]Oderisi's reflections about the fleeting nature of creative success seem to echo Psalm 90: 4-12: "For a thousand years in thy sight are but

I answered him, "Your true words fill my heart with holy humility and deflate my swollen pride. But who is it of whom you were speaking?"

"That is Provenzan Salvani," he answered. "He is here because he presumptuously thought that he could grasp all of Siena. So thus he has been going along, and so he goes, ever since he died; this is the coin with which one pays if one was too presumptuous."

I asked, "If a spirit who waits until the last moment of life before he repents then has to wait below here for as many years as he lived on earth (unless holy prayers help him along), how has this one managed to get here directly?"[12]

"When he was living in his highest glory," he answered, "of his own free will he stationed himself in the center of Siena, in spite of the shame of it, in order to deliver his friend from the agony of Charles's prison—although he trembled in every vein.[13] I won't tell more, and I know I

---

as yesterday when it is past, or as a watch in the night. Thou dost sweep men away; they are like a dream, like grass which is renewed in the morning; in the morning it flourishes and is renewed; in the evening it fades and withers....So teach us to number our days that we may get a heart of wisdom."

[12]Provenzan, who was beheaded in battle in 1269, had not repented before that time.

[13]When Provenzan's friend was captured by Charles of Anjou and in danger of execution, Provenzan posted himself in the marketplace of Siena and humbly begged for alms in order to pay the ransom. He was mortified, but he won his friend's release; and in doing so he won his own release from a long wait outside the gate of Purgatory. It is obvious that Oderisi foresaw that in a couple of years Dante would be exiled by his neighbors in Florence and forced into begging. The implication is that this painful and humiliating way of life would serve to diminish Dante's pride. (Contemporary readers need to remember that the word *pride* was not used as a synonym for healthy self-esteem until recently. Dante had both the sin of pride and the gift of self-esteem.)

haven't made it clear. But all too soon your neighbors' actions will enable you to understand the rest. His deed excused him from waiting down below."

CANTO TWELVE

Up Sacred Steps

In matching steps, like oxen which are yoked together, I moved along beside that heavy-burdened spirit so long as my kind teacher allowed it. But when he said, "Leave him and hurry along, for here it's good for each person to urge his boat along with all his might, with both sail and oar,"[1] then I made my body erect again for walking, although my thoughts remained bowed down and shriveled.[2]

I had moved along and was willingly following my teacher's steps, and both of us were showing how light-footed we were, when he said to me, "Cast your eyes downward; it will be worthwhile for you to pay attention to the pavement you walk upon."

So that the dead won't be forgotten, their flat tombs often show what they looked like; and that often causes a passerby to weep for them because of a stab of pity which only the compassionate feel. So I saw (but with better likeness, because of the Craftsman) stone figures engraved all over the road on the mountain ledge.[3]

---

[1] The reason for hurrying is eagerness for God's will, and the boat seems to stand for the soul on its journey toward holiness. John Ciardi suggests that the sail stands for prayer and the oar stands for personal effort.

[2] Dante is bowed down by awareness of his own sinful pride.

[3] In many European churches people have been buried under the pavement of the church floor, and worshippers can read who lies beneath their feet. (In Winchester Cathedral, for example, novelist Jane Austen is buried under the aisle.)

I saw on one side of the road the one who was created noblest of all creatures, falling like lightning from heaven.[4]

I saw on the other side Briareus, stricken by the celestial thunderbolt, lying heavily on the earth in his death chill.[5]

I saw Apollo, Mars and Athena still in armor by their father Jove, gazing at the giants' scattered limbs.[6]

I saw Nimrod at the foot of his great project, looking with bewilderment at his proud companions in Shinar.[7]

Ah Niobe, with what sad eyes I saw your image engraved on the road between your murdered children, seven on each side.[8]

Ah Saul, how you fell upon your sword and lay dead on Mount Gilboa, which never felt rain or dew again.[9]

Ah mad Arachne, I saw you already half turned into a spider, grieving upon the shreds of what you wove for your own misfortune.[10]

Ah Rehoboam, your image frightens no one, fleeing terrified in a chariot with no one pursuing.[11]

---

[4]In Luke 10:18 Jesus said, "I saw Satan fall like lightning from heaven." This is the first of thirteen stories of destructive pride that are carved on the pavement. The first four begin with "I saw." The next four begin with "Ah." The next four begin with "It showed."

[5]In Roman mythology, Briareus was one of the Titans (giants) who attacked Olympus in a foolish attempt to overthrow Jove.

[6]This family of gods defeated the giants with the help of Hercules.

[7]Genesis 11 tells of the building of the great Tower of Babel on the plain of Shinar, which resulted in God confusing the language of the people in order to break their power.

[8]Niobe, queen of Thebes, had boasted of her fourteen children in contrast to Jove's wife Latona who had only two. The gods killed all fourteen children with arrows, and Niobe was turned into a weeping statue.

[9]The story of Saul's pride and his eventual suicide when he was defeated by the Philistines is recorded in the book of I Samuel.

[10]Arachne was so proud of her weaving that she challenged the goddess Minerva to a contest, and was turned into a spider.

It showed — the hard pavement — how Alcmaeon made his mother pay a high price for her unlucky adornment.[12]

It showed how the sons of Sennacherib threw themselves upon him in the temple and left his dead body there.[13]

It showed the carnage Tomyris accomplished when she said to Cyrus, "You were bloodthirsty, so I'll give you your fill of blood."[14]

It showed how the Assyrians fled in dismay after Holofernes was assassinated, and the relics of that deed.[15]

> I saw Troy there overthrown in ashes.
> Ah Ilium — how low and vile
> It showed in the carved stone.[16]

---

[11]1 Kings 12 tells how Rehoboam, son of King Solomon, arrogantly disregarded his counselors, incited his subjects to rebellion, and then fled from them.

[12]Eriphyle was so vain that she betrayed her husband's hiding place for a certain gold necklace, and her son slew her in revenge. The gold necklace had been made with a curse upon it.

[13]2 Kings 18-19 tells the story of Sennacherib, the proud king of Assyria who was defeated when he insulted God and attacked Hezekiah, King of Judah. The angel of the Lord killed 185,000 Assyrian soldiers in their sleep. Later Sennacherib's sons cut him down with swords.

[14]Cyrus (560-529 B.C.), founder of the Persian Empire, murdered the son of Tomyris, Queen of Scythia. In revenge she had Cyrus killed and had his head dropped into a bucket of blood.

[15]The book of Judith in the Apocrypha tells how Judith, a beautiful Hebrew widow, tricked the arrogant enemy captain Holofernes into welcoming her to his tent for the night. When he was asleep she pounded a tent peg into his temple, then carried his head to her townspeople for public display. Thus the Hebrews defeated the Assyrians.

[16]Ilium is another name for the proud city of Troy. In this thirteenth example of destructive pride, Dante combined the three beginnings that he had been using ("I saw," "Ah," and "It showed.") In Italian the first

What master of brush or stylus could draw such lines
and shadings to amaze the wisest minds? The dead
seemed dead; the living, living. The actual witnesses never
saw these scenes I was walking on more clearly than I saw
them while I went along looking down.

But you, proud children of Eve, puff yourselves up
and hold your heads high, and don't bow down to look at
your evil path![17]

We had now gone farther around the mountain, and
the sun had traveled farther than my busy mind had
noticed, when he who was always alert to what's coming
said, "Raise your head. This is no time to be so absorbed.
Look at the angel who is getting ready to approach us.
See, the sixth handmaiden is finished with her day's
work.[18]

"Let reverence adorn your bearing and your face so
that he may be happy to send us on up. Remember that
this day won't ever dawn again!" By now I was so
accustomed to his warnings not to lose time that I could
not miss his subtle hint about it.

A beauteous creature came toward us, robed in white,
his countenance shimmering like a dawn star. He opened
his arms and spread wide his wings. He said, "Come. The
stairs are nearby, and climbing is easy now."[19]

---

letters of these three beginnings spell MAN, an acrostic pointing out that
pride and mankind are intimately connected.

[17]Dante is lamenting the blind foolishness of human pride. One
must figuratively bow one's head in humility in order to perceive
reality correctly.

[18]If each of the hour of the day is called a handmaiden, in April the
sixth handmaiden did her work between 11 a.m. and noon. It is now
shortly after noon on Easter Monday.

[19]This is the Angel of Humility; and the reason climbing becomes
easy now is that once pride is overcome, the other sins are easier to deal
with.

Few people respond to this summons. O human race, born to fly upward, why do you fall down at a puff of breeze?

He led us to where the rock was cut. There he brushed my forehead with his wings, then promised me a safe journey.[20]

When one ascends the mount where the church stands beyond the Rubicante Bridge, dominating the well-ruled city, on his right the steep slope is broken by a stairway that was built back in the days when measurements and public records were trustworthy.[21] That is how this slope, which plummets steeply down from the next ledge, is made easier; but on both sides lofty cliffs press close.

As we turned that direction, we heard voices singing "Blessed are the pure in spirit" in voices so sweet words can't describe it.[22] How different these entrances are from those in Hell! For here we were greeted with songs, and down there with savage howls.

Now we were climbing up the sacred steps, and I seemed to be much lighter than I had seemed on the level below. So I said, "Teacher, tell me, what heavy load has been lifted from me so that I notice almost no effort in going up?"

He answered, "When the P's remaining faintly on your forehead are completely erased like the one that is gone, your feet will be so full of enthusiasm that not only will

---

[20]When he brushed Dante's forehead, the Angel of Humility erased the P that stood for Pride.

[21]The church of San Miniato overlooks Florence, and an easy stairway leads to it up the hillside. Dante's use of the term "well-ruled" is ordinary sarcasm. His mention of untrustworthy measurements and account books refers to specific cases of fraud and graft that were scandals in Florence in his day.

[22]This benediction of the first ledge is from the Beatitudes, Matthew 5:3.

they feel no effort, but they will take delight in being directed upward."

Then I behaved like people who walk along with something on their head they don't know about, except that people's reactions make them suspicious—causing the hand to come to the rescue, so it searches and finds and accomplishes that which the eyes can't do.

With the fingers of my right hand spread out, I could feel only six of the letters that the angel with the keys had cut upon my forehead; and my leader was watching me and smiled.[23]

---

[23]Now Dante realizes that the angel that shimmered like a dawn star has erased the P that stood for pride from his forehead.

CANTO THIRTEEN

Blind Beggars

We came to the top of the stairway. And there, for the second time, the mountain—which frees us from evil as we climb—is cut back. There a ledge circles the mountain, like the first ledge except that the curve is sharper.[1] No soul is there, and no images can be seen. The face of the cliff is bare, and so is the path, both of them the dark gray color of the stone.

"If we were to wait here for people whom we can question," the poet said, "I'm afraid that it would mean too much delay." Then he stared into the sun, stepped forth on his right foot, and pivoted toward the right. "Precious light, whom I trust as I enter this new path, guide us as we need to be guided. You warm the world and give it light. If nothing directs us differently, sunbeams must always be our guide."[2]

Because of our eagerness, in a short time we had already gone what we would figure here as about a mile;[3] then we heard (but did not see) spirits flying toward us, inviting us courteously to a love feast.

---

[1] The curve of each ledge is sharper as one ascends the mountain because the circumference of the mountain gets smaller as one goes up.

[2] Virgil has not traveled in Purgatory before, so he does not know the way. He heads toward the afternoon sun because the sun is a symbol for God. He and Dante are on the north, sunny side of the mountain, and they will never circle it to the shady south side.

[3] Dante often gives specific details about space and time in *The Divine Comedy*, but in that spiritual dimension space and time are different from those on earth.

The first voice which flew by us said loudly, "They have no wine," and kept repeating it as it flew away.[4]

And before it had faded away entirely, another voice passed us crying "I am Orestes;" and it, also, did not stay.[5]

"Father," I said, "what are these voices?" And even as I was asking, a third one started saying "Love those who have harmed you."[6]

Then my good teacher said, "This circle lashes the sin of envy, and therefore the thong of the horse whip is made of love.[7] The sound of the harness must be quite different, and I think you will hear it before you reach the Pass of Pardon. But look very carefully through the air ahead of us, and you will see people sitting along the bank."

I opened my eyes wider than before; I looked ahead and saw souls in cloaks no different from the color of the stone. After we came a little closer, I heard their cry

---

[4]In John 2:3 Mary said this to Jesus to request wine for the wedding guests.

[5]According to tradition, when Orestes (son of the king of Mycenae in ancient Greece) was condemned to death, his friend Pylades tried to take his place by saying "I am Orestes." Charles Dickens echoed this event at the end of *A Tale of Two Cities*. In John 15:13 Christ says "Greater love has no one than this, that he lay down his life for his friends" (NIV).

[6]In Luke 6:27-28 Christ says "But I tell you who hear me: Love your enemies, do good to those who hate you, bless those who curse you, pray for those who mistreat you" (NIV).

[7]On each ledge in Purgatory there are two audio-visual object lessons, sometimes referred to as a bridle and a whip, used to guide people, like horses, in the right direction. The bridle consists of tragic Biblical and historical or mythological examples of a cardinal sin, and the whip consists of examples of the virtue that is the opposite of that sin.

"Mary, pray for us," and the cry "Michael and Peter and all saints."[8]

I don't believe that anywhere on earth today there is a man so hard that he would not be pierced with compassion at what I saw next. For when I came close enough to see their features clearly, heavy grief began running from my eyes. They seemed to be dressed in coarse haircloth;[9] each one was supporting the other on his shoulder, and all of them were leaning against the bank. Just like that, the blind without adequate provision sit on church porches on pardon days begging for their needs;[10] and one leans his head upon another, so that people will take pity not only for the sound of their words, but also for their looks — which plead just as much.

Just as the blind get no good from the sunlight, so the souls I was describing lack the gift of heaven's light because all their eyelids were stitched shut with iron wire — as men sometimes do to a wild hawk that won't settle down.[11] I felt I wronged them to go on looking at them when they couldn't look back, and so I turned to my wise counselor.

He knew well what my silence meant, and so he did not wait for my question, but said, "Speak to them, but be brief and to the point."

---

[8] The souls are chanting the Litany of the Saints, which addresses first the Trinity, then the Virgin Mary, then Michael and the other angels, St. Peter and the other apostles, and then the other saints. John Ciardi points out that the words "pray for us" rather than "pray for me" indicate turning from envy and growing in love.

[9] Coarse cloth made from goathair was painfully abrasive to the skin, which accounts for the term "wearing a hairshirt."

[10] The blind would gather on special holy days to beg for charity from churchgoers.

[11] Temporarily blindfolding a captured falcon with a hood or sealing its eyes with silk thread keeps it calm and relaxed so it can be tamed.

Virgil was walking beside me on the side of the ledge where one could fall off because there is no railing. On my other side were the praying souls who through the cruel stitches were shedding tears that trickled down their cheeks.[12]

I turned to them and said, "You people who are sure of seeing that high light which is your only desire, may grace quickly wash away the scum on your conscience so that the stream of memory may flow through you clean and clear. Now tell me, for I will treasure it, if any soul among you is Italian, and perhaps it will be good for him if I know that."

"My brother, every one of us is a citizen of the true city. You meant to ask if any of us lived his earthly pilgrimage in Italy."

It sounded to me as if this answer came from a bit farther along the way, and so I went over there to talk. Among the rest, I saw a soul that looked expectant because of the way its chin was lifted up like a blind person's.

"Spirit," I said, "you who have tamed yourself so that you may soar, if you are the one who answered me, tell me your origin or your name."[13]

"I was from Siena," she answered, "and with the others here I wash away my sinful life, weeping to Him for the gift of Himself. I was named Sapia, but I was not sapient;[14] and I took more pleasure in other people's misfortune than in my own good fortune.

---

[12]It is important to remember that these souls are here by choice, and when each one decides that he is ready, he will move on up the mountain.

[13]Dante continues his analogy about hawk-training, but now the hawk is choosing to be trained.

[14]Sapia's name sounds like sapient (wise), and she points out the irony of that.

"So that you won't think that I am exaggerating, listen and decide for yourself if I was insane as I say. When my life's arch was already descending, my townspeople were battling their enemies near Colle and I prayed for God's will to be done. They were defeated. They were reeling back in the bitter paths of flight, and seeing it I felt incomparable joy. So much, that I lifted up my bold face, crying to God 'Now I fear you no more,' as a blackbird responds to a brief bit of sunshine.[15]

"I sought peace with God near the end of my life, but I would not yet be able to pay off my sin with penitence if it were not for the fact that Peter Combseller remembered me in his holy prayers because in his charity he grieved for me.[16]

"But who are you, moving along and asking us about ourselves with your eyes not sewn shut, if I judge correctly, and breathing as you speak?"

"My eyes," I answered, "will be sealed here in the future, but for only a short time because they did not often look at people with envy. Greater far is my fear of the torture below us. My soul is anxious, for I already feel the burden down there weighing on me."[17]

---

[15]Sapia refers to an Italian fable about a happy blackbird that cries out foolishly during a warm spell in January, "I fear you no more, Lord, now that the winter is behind me." According to John Ciardi, Sapia resented her nephew Provenzano (see Canto 11) so much for surpassing her husband in his rise to power that when he was beheaded in battle in 1269 she reportedly cried, "Now God, do what you will with me, and do me any harm you can, for after this I shall live happily and die content."

[16]It was the prayers of the eccentric but saintly Peter Combseller that enabled Sapia to enter Purgatory without waiting for many years below St. Peter's Gate.

[17]Dante is indicating that he expects to return to Purgatory for purification from the stain of past sins after his death and dreads the time he will spend on the first ledge under a slab of stone because of his pride. But when he wrote this passage sometime between 1310 and

And she answered, "Then who has led you up here to us, if you expect to return below?"

I answered, "He who is with me and hasn't said a word. I am alive, blessed soul, so tell me if you want me to run an errand for you on my mortal feet back home."

"Oh, this is so unusual that it must mean God loves you," she answered, "so bless me sometimes with your prayers. And I beg you by all you desire most, if you ever set your feet in Tuscany, that you tell my family the news about me. You will find them among the foolish crowd who put their trust in Talamone and will lose more hope there than in their search for Diana; but there the admirals will lose the most."[18]

1317 he was no doubt thinking of the torture of exile that weighed him down starting in 1302 and painfully humbled his pride in his lifetime.

[18]Sapia can foresee that the leaders of Siena will buy the small port of Talamone in 1303 and try to turn it into a major harbor by dredging and building there. (Talamone is on the west coast of Italy 80 miles south of Siena.) Silt from the creek made the expensive dredging futile, and local malaria killed the admirals who were supervising. Siena had already invested in a futile 1295 search for a phantom underground stream named Diana. Siena's costly misjudgments were obviously no more foolish than Sapia's costly misjudgments had been.

CANTO FOURTEEN

The Cry of Cain

"Who is this who walks around our mountain before death has set him loose, and opens and shuts his eyes when he pleases?"

"I don't know who he is, but I know that he's not alone. Ask him, since you are closer to him, and be sure to address him courteously so that he will speak."[1]

Thus on my right two spirits were leaning against each other and talking about me. Then they held up their faces to speak to me, and one said, "O soul that is heading toward heaven while still wearing your body, for love's sake comfort our minds and tell us where you come from and who you are. For you astonish us by what is granted to you, since this never happened before."

I answered, "Through the heart of Tuscany there flows a stream which starts in Falterona, and a hundred miles is not enough to complete it. From its banks I bring this body. To tell you my name would be useless, for my name is not yet famous."

"If I catch your meaning with my understanding," said the first one who spoke, "you are talking about the Arno."

And the other said to him, "Why did he avoid the name of the river as one avoids the name of something horrible?"

---

[1] All the souls who cannot see Dante can tell a great deal from the sound of his breathing and his footsteps. The second speaker is evidently timid, because he is close enough to speak to Dante if he wants to.

Then the soul who was asked this question answered, "I don't know, but it is surely fitting for the name of such a valley to perish. From its beginning in the rugged mountains from which Pelorus was cut off, outsoaring most other mountains,[2] all the way to where it pours itself out to replace the water which the sun pulls up from the sea in order to fill the rivers, virtue is chased away by everyone as if it were an enemy—in fact, a snake—either because the area is jinxed, or else because of evil family traditions. As a result, inhabitants of that wretched valley have so degenerated that it seems as if Circe has them in her pen.[3]

"It first finds its feeble way among filthy hogs, more worthy of acorns than of food for humans. Then, descending, it finds curs snarling more than their weakness warrants, and it scornfully turns aside its snout.[4] It goes on down, and the larger it grows, the more this accursed and doomed ditch finds the dogs grown into wolves. Having plunged down many deep gorges, it finds foxes so full of fraud that they fear no attempt to trap them.

"I won't stop here, although someone is listening to us—and it may do him good to recall someday my true prophecy.[5] I see your grandson, who becomes a hunter of

---

[2]The Arno River starts at Falterona, the summit of the Tuscan Apennine mountain range. Pelorus is a mountain in Sicily that is separated from the Apennines by water but is geologically part of that mountain range.

[3]In *The Odyssey* Homer told how the beautiful witch Circe enchanted men and turned them into hogs. Dante says that the people of Casentino are now like hogs, those of the Aretines are like curs, those of Florence are like greedy wolves, and those of Pisa are like crafty foxes.

[4]The Arno River, likened to a beast, turns eastward three miles north of Arezzo.

[5]At this point Guido's flash of prophecy obviously shows him that Dante is from Florence.

those wolves by the fierce river and strikes terror in them all. He sells their living flesh, and then the old beast slaughters them for sport. He destroys their life and destroys his own honor. Blood-spattered, he comes out of the sad forest. He leaves it such that it won't grow back to what it was in a thousand years."[6]

Just as a listener's face looks stricken when terrible news is announced, whatever the source of the catastrophe—so I saw the soul who had listened, stunned with sorrow soon after it took in the words. The speaker's words and the listener's face made me long to know their names, and so I asked prayerfully.

Thus it was that the spirit who spoke first to me began again, "You want me to do for you what you would not do for me; but since God's favor shines so brightly in you, I won't be grudging. Know that I was Guido del Duca.

"My blood was so aflame with envy that if I happened to see another man rejoicing, you would have seen my face turn livid. That's what I sowed, and now I am reaping straw.[7] O humankind, why do you set your heart where it is impossible to share with others?

"This is Rinieri, the glory and honor of the Calboli family, where there has been no heir worthy of him.[8] And it is not only his family that is stripped of the goodness of truth and chivalry—between the river Po and the Apennine mountains, and the seashore and the river Reno.

---

[6]The sad forest is Florence, and the bloody hunter is Fulcieri da Calboli, who was the elected ruler in 1302, when Dante was exiled.

[7]Guido is referring to Galatians 6:7, "Do not be deceived. God cannot be mocked. A man reaps what he sows" (NIV). No one wants to reap straw, because it is not food.

[8]The fact that Rinieri and Guido del Duca have been leaning on each other shows that they are now learning love in place of envy. The fact that Guido praises Rinieri when he introduces him to Dante shows that he can now enjoy admiring other people rather than fearing their merits.

For the land within those four boundaries is so choked with poison weeds that it would be hard now to root them out with years of cultivation.[9]

"Where is good Lizio? Arrigo Mainardi? Pier Traversaro? Guido di Carpigna? You people of Romagna are all bastards now! When will Bologna grow another Fabbro? When will Faneza grow another Bernardin di Fosco, noble offshoot of a humble plant?

"Don't be surprised, man from Tuscany, if I weep when I remember Guido da Prata and Ugolin d' Azzo, who lived among us, Federico Tignoso and his circle, the Traversaro family, and the Anastagi (both without any heirs). The ladies and the knights, the work and sports which brought us together in love and courtesy — there where hearts have now grown so wicked.[10]

"Brettinoro, why don't you just disappear, since your nobility have left along with many others, to escape evil?[11] Bagnacaval does well to have no sons, and Catrocaro does ill and Conio worse because they bothered to breed worthless noblemen. The Pagani family will do well when their fiend is gone, but not well enough to restore their reputation.[12] Your name is safe, Ugolin de' Fantolin, since

---

[9]The rest of Guido's conversation is about prominent people who lived in Romagno, the area that he has just described. Like Dante, he grieves over the ruin of his beloved homeland. It is important that he wants to praise many of his fellow countrymen.

[10]Dorothy Sayers observes, "To the penitent Guido, looking back upon his life, the gay companionship which in the old days filled him with envy and uncharitableness now appears a thing full of happiness, to be wistfully regretted."

[11]Brettinoro was the small town where Guido was born.

[12]The fiendish Count Maginardo would die in 1302 and then his family would have decent leadership again, but their name would be permanently stained by him.

there is no more chance for an heir to blacken it by dragging it down.[13]

"But now go on your way, man from Tuscany, because I would far rather weep than talk, now that our conversation has wrung my heart."

We knew that those dear souls could hear how we left, and their silence made us sure we were going in the right direction.

As soon as we were journeying on alone, a voice that split the air like lightning hit us suddenly, crying "Whoever finds me will kill me!"[14] And it rolled away like a thunderclap in a cloudburst.

As soon as our ears got back to normal, a second voice spoke with such a loud crash that it was like thunder following thunder: "I am Aglauros, who was turned to stone."[15] At that I stepped backward, not forward, and huddled close to the poet.

The air became quiet all around us, and he said to me, "That was the iron bit of the rein which should keep humans in place. But you people gulp down the bait, and when the Old Adversary pulls you in to him, then neither horse rein nor falcon call is apt to help you.

"The heavens call to you and encircle you with never-ending splendors, but your eyes are glued to the ground. Therefore, He who knows all things must strike you."[16]

---

[13] Both of virtuous Ugolino's sons had died young.

[14] The story of Cain is found in Genesis 4. Cain jealously murdered his brother Abel, and when God sent him into exile he cried out that it was more than he could bear. He was not, in fact, killed by anyone, because God put a mark of protection on him.

[15] In Greek mythology, Aglauros was a princess of Athens. Her bitter jealousy of her sister caused her to break her promise to the god Mercury. As a result, he turned her to stone.

[16] In a medley of mixed metaphors (horse's bit, fish's bait, call to a tame falcon), Virgil points out that humans are so spiritually stupid that God must act harshly to save them from Satan.

The Stoning of Stephen
Gustave Doré (Canto 15)

CANTO FIFTEEN

Toward the Western Sun

The number of hours between daybreak and nine a.m. when one can see the sphere that always see-saws like a child at play — that is the number of hours of daylight that were left to us now before sunset.[1] It was vespers there,[2] and here in Italy it would have been midnight. The sun's rays were hitting us square on the bridge of the nose, because we had moved far enough around the mountain that now we were heading due west.

Then I felt my face hit by far more radiance than before, and something unknown dazed me. Therefore I raised my hands above my eyes and made a shade to shield me from the glare.

When a ray of light bounces off the water or from a mirror, it ascends at an off-angle just like the one by which it descended (and is just as far from the vertical line of a falling stone again, but now on the other side) — as both experiment and calculation can prove. So it was that I

---

[1]This amounts to an easy riddle. What time of day is as far from sunset as 9:00a.m. is from sunrise? The answer is obviously 3:00p.m. (Unfortunately, where Daylight Savings Time has been adopted recently it destroys the symmetry of the day; therefore many people no longer realize that noon meant the apex of the sun's daily journey across the sky, the exact midoint between sunrise and sunset.)

[2]Vespers is the three-hour period from 3:00 p.m. to 6:00 p.m., and Dante is repeating his point that in Purgatory it was 3:00 p.m.

seemed to be struck by reflected light right in front of me, which my eyes had to avoid.[3]

"What is that light, kind Father, from which I can't shade my eyes enough, and which seems to be moving toward us?"

"Don't wonder if the heavenly family still dazzles you," he answered. "It's a messenger who comes to invite us to go on up. Eventually such a sight won't be too hard, but will be as much joy to you as nature has enabled you to feel."

When we had reached the blessed angel, with a glad voice he said, "Enter here! This stairway is far less steep than the others."[4]

We were already climbing up past him, when we heard "Blessed are the merciful"[5] sung behind us, and "Rejoice, you who have overcome."[6]

---

[3]Dante has just described a fundamental law of optics. The sun is directly in front of him, and the brilliant new source of light is also right in front of him. Modern readers must remember that before electrical technology, the source of additional bright light on a sunny day was always a reflection of sunlight. In a spiritual sense, an angel reflects God's light on earth.

[4]This is the angel that is the opposite of envy. He is often called the Angel of Mercy, but John Ciardi calls him the Angel of Love for Others, and Dorothy Sayers calls him the Angel of Generosity.

[5]They heard this phrase from Matthew 5:7 sung in Latin. Dorothy Sayers says that the Latin word *misericordes* is wider in meaning than our English word *merciful* and might be better translated "tender-hearted," "sympathetic," or "generous-minded." This is what Thomas Aquinas meant when he wrote, "Envy is the direct opposite of mercy... for the envious man is saddened by his neighbour's prosperity, whereas the merciful man is saddened by his neighbour's misfortune..."

[6]This may echo three Bible verses: Matthew 5:12, "Rejoice and be glad, because great is your reward in heaven..." (RSV); Romans 12:21, "Do not be overcome by evil, but overcome evil with good" (NIV); and Revelation 2:7, "...To him who overcomes I will give the right to eat from the tree of life, which is in the paradise of God" (NIV).

My teacher and I, we two alone, were climbing up; and I thought that I might as well be profiting from conversation. So I addressed him, asking, "What did the spirit from Romagna mean when he referred to 'impossible to share with others'?"

Then he answered me, "He knows the harm in his own worst fault, and so no one should be surprised if he attacks it, hoping it will cause less grief. Whenever your desires are centered where your portion will be less if it is shared with others, then envy pumps the bellows of your sighs. But if heavenly love is what you desire, the fear in your heart will evaporate. For the more there are who say 'ours,' the more good each one of them has, and the more love blazes in the holy dwelling place."[7]

"I am hungrier for an answer now than if I hadn't asked," I said, "and I'm more perplexed. How can something good be divided up so that when more people share it, everyone gets a larger amount than if only a few people share it?"[8]

He answered me, "Because you are thinking only about worldly things, you see darkness when you look at light. That infinite and inexpressible Good in heaven springs

---

[7]The spirit from Romagna, Guido del Duca, had railed against envy because it was his besetting sin. Envy puts a person into a basically fearful competition with others and creates chronic anxiety about not getting enough or not keeping enough. An envious person feels cheated and deprived (he groans or sighs) when someone else prospers, because of inordinate concern about allocation of resources in his own favor. No matter how rich he is, he suffers from the threat of deprivation. The opposite condition is that of a person who flows with love and cares about everyone's welfare as much as his own. Loving people tend to think of "ours" rather than "mine." This spiritual light somehow reflects in heaven and increases the brightness there, as a mirror can reflect sunlight and increase the brightness in a spot on earth.

[8]Here Dante seems to be referring to Christ's miracle recorded in Matthew 14::17, Mark 6:38, Luke 9:13, and John 6:9, in which a little food was greatly multiplied by sharing.

toward love as light darts toward a bright surface. Where there is love, that Good adds to the love, so that wherever love exists, eternal Good multiplies itself. And the more souls are loving there, the better they love and the more love there is; and like mirrors they all multiply the brightness.

"If my answer still doesn't satisfy your hunger, you will see Beatrice later and she will free you from this and any other unsatisfied longing. Now keep striving, so that soon the other five wounds will be erased by sadness the same as two already are."[9]

As I was about to say, "This answer satisfies me!" I realized I was on the next ledge, and my eager eyes struck me silent.

There I felt myself suddenly caught up into an ecstatic vision where I saw a crowd in a temple. A woman near the entrance, with the tender manner of a mother, was saying, "Son, why have you treated us like this? Your father and I have been anxiously searching for you."[10]

Then there appeared to me another woman, her cheeks flowing with the water distilled by grief when it is driven upward by great rage, and she was saying, "Pisistratus, if you are ruler of the city that the gods fought to name, where knowledge sparkles, then take vengeance on those bold arms that embraced our daughter!"

---

[9]After some dizzying words about the heavenly economy, no doubt beyond Dante's comprehension, Virgil cheers him with a promise that Beatrice is ahead and the news that another "P" has disappeared from his forehead. That is something Dante can understand.

[10]Luke 2:41-50 tells the story of a trip that Mary and Joseph took from Nazareth to Jerusalem when Jesus was twelve years old. In his vision Dante saw the scene when Mary found her missing son in the temple courtyard. Readers are expected to realize that Jesus answered "Didn't you know that I had to be in my Father's house?" and that although she did not understand him, she treasured the event in her heart. Dante used this as an example of meekness toward family.

And the ruler appeared to me to answer her kindly and gently, with a peaceful face, "If we punished one who loves us, what would we do to one who does us harm?"[11]

Then I saw people enflamed with anger, murdering a young man with stones and yelling at each other over and over, "Kill, kill!" And I saw him collapsing toward the ground because death was weighing him down. But his eyes were like gates open to heaven, and he was praying to the high Lord during all this torture with a beseeching look, that God would forgive these enemies.[12]

When my consciousness of my real surroundings returned, I recognized my not-false hallucinations for what they were.

My leader, who saw me acting like a man aroused from sleep, said, "What's the matter with you that you cannot control yourself, but have staggered along for more than a mile and a half with your eyes half shut, like someone overcome with wine or sleepiness?"

"Oh my dear father," I answered, "if you listen to me I will tell you what appeared to me when my legs were not my own."

He said, "If you wore a hundred masks on your face, you couldn't hide even your smallest thoughts from me. What you saw was so that you have no excuse not to open your heart to the waters of peace which pour from the eternal fountain.[13] I didn't ask 'What ails you?' as if I were someone who sees only through his eyes that quit

---

[11]Pisistratus was a usurper who ruled Athens wisely and kindly from 560-527 B.C. A young man who wished to marry his daughter impulsively embraced her in public, which outraged her mother. But Pisistratus forgave the young man instead of killing him. Dante used this as an example of meekness toward friends.

[12]The stoning of Stephen is described in Acts 7:54-60. This is a classic example of meekness toward one's enemies.

[13]Jeremiah 2:13 and 17:13 refers to God as the fountain of living waters.

when the body quits. I asked in order to strengthen your steps; that's how sluggards must be urged along who are slow to make good use of their waking time when awareness returns."[14]

We were journeying on into the evening, straining our eyes ahead as far as we could into the evening and the bright rays of the low sun. And then, little by little, a cloud of smoke as black as night was rolling toward us, with no way for us to escape it. It took away the pure air and our sight.

---

[14]John Ciardi says that Virgil is really urging Dante to apply the three visions to himself because Dante is more wrathful than meek by nature.

CANTO SIXTEEN

Dark Smoke

Neither the gloom of Hell nor a night stripped of its heavenly bodies under a poverty-stricken sky—as darkened by cloud as sky can be—ever wrapped my face in such a thick and gritty veil as that smoke which now enveloped us, for it didn't even allow my eyes to stay open. Therefore my wise and faithful escort drew close and placed my hand on his shoulder.

Just as a blind man follows his guide so that he won't get lost or run into something that might hurt him or even kill him, so I made my way through the foul and filthy air, listening to my guide say over and over, "Be careful not to let go of me!"[1]

I heard voices, and each one seemed to pray for peace and mercy to the Lamb of God that takes away our sins. The prayers all began with "Agnus Dei," and each word and phrase was spoken by the voices together, so they were in perfect unison.[2]

---

[1] In Canto 7 of *The Inferno*, the souls of the angry were stuck in slime, lamenting, 'We sulked in the sweet air that was gladdened by the sun, our hearts sullen and smoky within us.' Here in Purgatory Dante has come to the souls that are being saved from their smoky anger, the only place after Hell where Dante uses the Italian word *sozzo*, meaning *filthy*. Dorothy Sayers points out that anger is like smoke because it makes people blind to what is right and also suffocates natural feelings and responses. John Ciardi points out that Dante needs to hang on to Virgil in the smoke, just as we need to hang on to Reason (clear thinking, wisdom) when we find ourselves blinded by anger.

[2] "Agnus Dei" is Latin for the Lamb of God, and the prayer here is "O Lamb of God, that takest away the sins of the world, have mercy upon us; grant us Thy peace." This is a prayer in the Roman Catholic

"Teacher, are these spirits I hear?" I asked.

He answered me, "You guess correctly, and they are untying the knot of anger."

"Now who are you, cutting through our smoke and talking about us as if you were still living in calendar time?" a voice asked.

At that, my teacher said to me, "Answer him, and ask if this is the way for us to go on up."

I said, "Creature, cleansing yourself in order to return in beauty to Him who made you, if you come with us you will hear about a marvel."

"I will follow you as far as I'm allowed," it answered, "and if the smoke doesn't let us see, our hearing will keep us together instead."

Then I began, "In these wrappings that death will someday dissolve, I am traveling upward—and came here through the anguish of Hell. If God has received me so far in his grace that He chooses to let me behold Heaven in a way unheard of in modern times,[3] then don't keep secret who you were before you died, but tell me. Tell me also if I am heading toward the stairs, and your words shall be our guide."

"I was a Lombard, and I was called Marco. I knew the world and loved the values that men no longer honor. You

---

mass based upon John 1:29: "The next day John saw Jesus coming toward him and said, 'Look, the Lamb of God, who takes away the sin of the world' "(NIV). Spirits of the wrathful have a special need for mercy and peace and special need to pray in unison after the divisiveness of their lives.

[3]This is the marvel that Dante offered to reveal: that in his living body he has come through Hell and is traveling up to Heaven. No one alive has seen Heaven since St. Paul did so almost 1300 years earlier. At the beginning of Canto 2 of *The Inferno*, Dante had tried to back out of this journey and said, "I am no Aeneas, I am no Paul. No one thinks me worthy of the trip, especially myself. Therefore, if I went through with this journey, I fear it would be absolute folly."

are heading right to go up the mountain." Thus he
answered, and added, "I hope that you will pray for me
when you are up above."[4]

I said to him, "On my honor I promise to do what you
ask of me, but I am going to burst with a certain problem
if I don't let it loose. At first it was a simple problem, but
now it is compounded by what you said, which I'm sure
that I'm correct to link to what was said to me elsewhere.[5]

"The world is indeed devoid of all virtue, as your
words said to me; it is loaded down and covered with sin.
But I beg you to tell me the cause of all this, so that I may
see it and show it to others. For some say the cause is in
the stars, and some, here on earth."[6]

First he heaved a deep sigh, which grief squeezed into
"Oh, my." Then he began, "Brother, the world is blind,
and you certainly come from it. You who are alive
attribute everything to the stars, as if they swept
everything along with them by force.[7] If it were so, free

---

[4]Marco Lombardo is forgotten except in Dante's tale. He was
obviously a good-hearted man with a hot temper.

[5]Dante is still thinking about Guido del Duca's long, bitter
monologue in Canto 14 about the wickedness of Italy. Guido was
blinded like a falcon on the ledge of envy, and Marco is blinded by
smoke on the ledge of wrath.

[6]Dorothy Sayers points out that if the stars were responsible for sin,
it would not really be sin. Dante's question is ironic on the ledge where
anger is being treated. "It is useless, on the one hand, to be angry with
anyone for doing what he could not help doing; and on the other, [if we
have no free will] the anger itself is merely a mechanical gesture, as
much determined as the behaviour which appears to provoke it."

[7]Dante put astrologers in Hell with sorcerers in the Canto 20 of the
Inferno, for trying to predict and control the future by calculating the
positions of the planets. But he accepted the idea that the heavenly
bodies are part of our environment with influence upon us. In Marco's
insistence that the stars do not rule us, Dante is refuting much more than
popular astrology. As Dorothy Sayers puts it, "When he speaks of the
stars as [not being] the sole origin of causation he means by that exactly

will would be destroyed, and it would be unfair to reward goodness with joy and evil with sorrow.

"The stars[8] get your impulses started (I don't say all of your impulses, but suppose I did...); you have received light in order to tell good from evil, and Free Will which, after it endures the effort of its first battles against the stars, eventually wins the victory if it is well nourished.

"You who are alive submit in your freedom to a greater power and a better nature, which has given you a mind that the stars can't overpower. Therefore, if today the world has gone astray, the cause is in you and in you it should be sought.[9] Now I'll explore this matter for you.

"The simple, tender soul comes forth from the hands of the one who loved her fondly before she existed, like a little child who laughs and cries and plays and knows nothing except that, having sprung from a joyous creator, she eagerly turns toward whatever delights her. First she tastes the flavor of some little pleasure; then she is entranced and runs after it unless a guide or boundary-wall channels her love.[10]

---

what the modern determinist means by saying that all events in the universe, including human behaviour, follow each other in inevitable sequence as the result of physical interaction of the atoms composing it. A man is what he is and does what he does because the course of nature threw him up at such and such a time and under such and such conditions..."

[8]"The stars" here stand for all that is imposed by heredity and environment.

[9]Shakespeare's version of this statement is found in *Julius Caesar*, Act 1, Scene 2: "The fault, dear Brutus, is not in our stars, But in ourselves, that we are underlings."

[10]Susan Noakes considers this analysis of the human condition and love the heart of the *Comedy*. As she points out, Dante placed it at the midpoint of the *Comedy*, in the sixteenth canto of *Purgatory*. (The following cantos expand upon it.) See "The Double Misreading of Paolo and Francesca" by Susan Noakes in *Dante*, edited by Harold Bloom (New York: Chelsea House Publishers, 1986).

"Therefore it was necessary to have law as a boundary and necessary to have a ruler who could see at least the tower of the true city. The laws are there, but who has a hand that will enforce them? No one. The shepherd who leads may chew the cud, but his hooves are not divided.[11] When the people see that their guide aims only at satisfying his own greed, they feed on that also and seek nothing better.

"You can easily see that evil leadership has made the world evil, and not natural forces. Rome, which made the world decent, used to have two suns which lit up two roads, the road of the world and the road of God.[12] But now one sun has quenched the other. The sword has merged with the shepherd's staff. Joined together, they are bound to go bad, because then neither one fears the other. If you don't believe me, look at the ear of grain, because every plant is known by the seed it produces.[13]

"Over the land watered by the Adige and the Po rivers, worth and courtesy used to be found before Frederick was

---

[11]Dante is condemning the chaos of Italian government in his day. The ruler was the emperor, and the true city is the City of God; an emperor should at least see the tower (be committed to justice). The shepherd who leads (poorly) is Pope Boniface VIII, likened to an "unclean animal" in Leviticus 11:3. John Ciardi says, "Pope Boniface may ruminate, allegorically 'chew the cud' of the Scriptures and God's law, but he does not recognize the need for 'cloven hooves,' the separation or cleft between spiritual and temporal powers."

[12]According to Dorothy Sayers, the empire that Dante admired was that of Constantine, Theodosius, and Justinian (circa 300-565 A.D.). They are commemorated in the glorious mosaics at Ravenna, where Dante completed *Purgatory* and wrote all of *Paradise*.

[13]Dante saw theocracy as inevitably corrupt. His warning seems to echo Matthew 7:15-16: "Watch out for false prophets. They come to you in sheep's clothing, but inwardly they are ferocious wolves. By their fruit you will recognize them" (NIV).

opposed.[14] But now anyone who would be embarrassed to talk with good men, or even to be near any, may travel there quite safely.

"It's true that there are three old men there through whom the old times rebuke the new, and they feel that God is very slow to take them on to a better life: Corrado da Palazzo, and good Gerard, and Guido da Castel— well-named by the French "the honest Lombard.""[15]

"Teach from now on that the Church of Rome, by mixing two kinds of power in herself, falls into the mud and befouls herself and her load."

"My friend Marco," I said, "you reason well! Now I see why Levi's sons were not allowed to inherit wealth.[16] But what Gerard is that who you say is a relic of the vanished breed, to put to shame this degenerate age?"

"Either your language tricks me or your words are testing me," he answered, "for you speak Tuscan, and yet seem to know nothing about Good Gerard. I know no other name for him, unless I identify him by his daughter Gaia.[17]

"God be with you, for I come no farther with you. See the light beaming through the smoke and growing bright!

---

[14]The land described by Marco is Lombardy in Northern Italy, torn by strife between Emperor Frederick II and the Pope.

[15]Guido da Castel was noted for his generosity and hospitality. The French called Italians Lombards and considered them shrewd and greedy, and so their praise for Guido was an especially strong tribute.

[16]In Numbers 18:20 God told Aaron that the men of the tribe of Levi, set aside as priests, would not inherit wealth: "I am your share and your inheritance among the Israelites" (NIV). Dante sees the wisdom of this in light of the worldly corruption of the Roman Catholic Church.

[17]Gherardo da Cammino, who died in 1306, was so well known that Marco thought Dante must be joking about not knowing his name. It seems that Good Gerard's daughter Gaia was notorious for her loose morals.

The angel is there, and I should leave before he sees me."[18]
So he turned back and heard me no more.

---

[18]Marco does not mean that he is hiding from the angel. He has
come to the edge of the smoke cloud and knows he belongs back inside
it until he is thoroughly cleansed of anger. It seems obvious that both
Marco and Dante need to be cleansed of their dark inner smoke-cloud
of righteous anger, which is toxic to them rather than to the evil-doers
who enrage them.

CANTO SEVENTEEN

Caught by Nightfall

Reader, if a mountain mist has ever caught you through which you could see only as moles do, through their skin,[1] remember how the disk of the sun enters weakly through the moist, thick vapors as they begin to melt away. Then your imagination will easily arrive at how I beheld the sun again, which was now setting.

So, matching my footsteps with the trusty steps of my teacher, I came forth from the smoke cloud to see the sunshine, although the light had already died on the seashore far below.

Fantasy—which snatches us out of ourselves sometimes so that we are conscious of nothing, even if a thousand trumpets blast around us—who moves you, if the senses show you nothing? A light moves you which is formed in Heaven, either self-generated or sent down by the will of God.

In my imagination I saw some of the cruelty of that one[2] who was changed into the bird that most delights in singing. And at this point my consciousness was so turned inward that I was oblivious to anything outside myself. Next, into my fantasy there fell the image of a

---

[1] Moles have extremely small eyes, reportedly protected by a membrane through which they see dimly.

[2] In classical legend, King Tereus of Thrace violated his sister-in-law Philomena and cut out her tongue to keep her from telling his wife Procne. When Procne found out, in her evil wrath she killed her son Itys and fed him to Tereus. The gods turned the trio into birds, and according to the version that Dante used, Procne became a nightingale.

man with a fierce and scornful face being crucified, and near him were the great Ahasuerus, Esther his queen, and Mordecai the just, whose words and deeds were true.[3] That image disappeared like a bubble that bursts and becomes a drop of water, and in its place I saw a maiden weeping loudly. "My Queen, why did you allow wrath to cause your suicide? You killed yourself over Lavinia's loss, and thus you lost Lavinia. I am weeping for your death, Mother, not for another's."[4]

As sleep shatters when new light suddenly strikes the sleeper's eyelids, yet quivers briefly before it dies away, so the vision fell away when a brilliant light beyond any we know struck my face. I turned to see where I was, and a voice that drove everything else from my mind said "Here one rises." I was overwhelmed with unquenchable desire to see whoever spoke, face to face. But as it is when the sun dims our eyes and is veiled from our sight by its excessive brilliance, so I lacked the power.

"This is a heavenly spirit[5] that points us to our upward way without our asking and is hidden by its own light. It treats us as men treat themselves, for one who sees a need and waits for the request has partially refused to help. Now let's accept the invitation with our feet and try to make the climb before nightfall, or else we will have to delay until sunrise."

---

[3]In the Old Testament book of Esther, a high official named Haman was hanged because in his rage against faithful Mordecai he ordered all the Jews in Persia to be destroyed. Queen Esther saved Mordecai by bravely appealing to King Ahasuerus.

[4]In Homer's *Aeneid*, when Amatus mistakenly thought that her daughter Lavinia's intended husband was killed by Aeneus, she impulsively hanged herself in wrath and despair. From Dante's point of view, Amatus was rebelling against God's will.

[5]This is the Angel of Meekness; Dante will eventually be able to see him in Heaven.

Thus my Teacher spoke, and we turned toward the stairway; and as soon as I was on the first step I felt as if my face were fanned by a wing, and I heard someone say "Blessed are the peacemakers, who have no evil wrath."[6]

Now the last sunrays were so high above us on the mountain that already the stars were shining here and there. "Strength, why are you deserting me?" I said silently, because my legs felt shackled.

We stood at the top of the stairs, stuck like a ship run aground. I listened awhile in case I could hear anything in this new circle, then turned to my Teacher and said, "Dear Father, which kind of sin is washed away in this circle? Although our feet are stopped, don't stop your teaching."

He said to me, "The love of goodness that fails to function is repaired here. Here the unused oar starts to row again. For you to see that clearly, pay attention and you shall gather some good fruit from our waiting here."

He began, "Neither the Creator nor his creatures ever existed without love, either instinctual or conscious love. Instinctual love is never blameworthy; but conscious love may be wrong because of a wrong love object or too much or too little love for a right love object. When it is directed toward Eternal Good or to temporary good in suitable degree, love is never wrong. But when it aims at evil or aims at good too strongly or too weakly, the creature is working against its Maker. Thus you should understand that love is the seed of all your virtues and all your faults.[7]

---

[6]This Beatitude is from Matthew 5:9. (Evil wrath is different from righteous indignation.) The Angel of Meekness has erased the third P from Dante's forehead.

[7]As Dorothy Sayers points out, "lesser goods" are all those legitimate objects of love which are not God. "If any one of them is preferred before God, then the love errs by excess; further, a right order must be observed among them; e. g. to put love of money before love of

"So far as love can never disregard the welfare of the thing it loves, all things are safe from self-hatred; and because no one can imagine existing apart from a Higher Power, no one can wish harm to the Higher Power. It follows, then, if my analysis is correct, that we can only love the evil that befalls our fellow creatures; and this love of evil arises in three ways.

"First is the person who hopes that some successful person's misfortune will increase his own chance for success; thus he hopes to see another cast down.

"Second, there is the person who fears that someone else's progress may cut into his own power, popularity, honor and fame; thus he prefers that others should fail.

"Third, there is the one who so resents the wrongs he has endured that he lusts for revenge and seeks to harm another.

"Below us, this threefold love of evil is repented. Next I want you to understand the love of goodness that is out of proportion. We all vaguely sense that we long for blissful rest for our souls, and that is our true goal. If our love for our true goal is lukewarm, however, this ledge is where we pay the penalty.[8]

"Earthly good is not the source of everlasting joy; God is the fruit and root of all other goodness. Inordinate love of lesser good is repented in the three circles above us; but I won't describe those three divisions because you may observe them for yourself."

---

one's neighbour would also be an error by excess. But provided that 'due measure' is kept there is no sin in loving pleasant things."

[8] Lower Purgatory included penitents on three ledges: the proud with heavy stones, the envious with sealed eyes, and the wrathful in smoke. Now Dante and Virgil are in Middle Purgatory, where the fourth ledge is for those who are spiritually slothful.

CANTO EIGHTEEN

Runners' Marathon

The great Teacher had ended his lecture and was looking intently into my face to see if I was satisfied. Although I was thirsty for more answers, I kept quiet, telling myself that too many questions might irritate him. But he, true father that he was, sensed my secret desire and encouraged me to speak up.

I said, "Teacher, my sight improves so much in your light that I see clearly all that your words imply or explain. Therefore I beg you, dear and gentle Father, that you define love for me, to which you credit every good and evil deed."

"Look at me with the sharp eyes of your understanding," he said, "and the folly of blind guides will become clear. The soul, which is created prone to love, is quickly drawn to anything that pleases it. From a real object, you receive a mental image that attracts your soul, and if your soul is attracted, that is love; and love binds you naturally with bonds of pleasure. Then as fire moves upward, which is its nature, so the soul in love, which is a spiritual motion, does not rest until love is fulfilled.

"Now be sure to comprehend how far from the truth are those who claim that every act of love is praiseworthy because, truly, love is basically good material. But not every object made out of good wax is a good object."

"Your words and my eagerness to learn reveal what love is. But now I have a greater problem. For if love comes to us from outside ourselves and is our soul's only means of moving about, we are not responsible for going straight or crooked."

He said to me, "I can take you only as far as logic will go; beyond that point, wait for Beatrice's help, for it's a matter of faith. Every earthly soul that is more than material and yet manifest in material form has some free will. This can't be directly seen, but we see evidence for it in its results—as green leaves tell us a plant is alive. Therefore, no one can know how he was first enlightened or the source of his deep longing for God, which is like the bee's inborn desire to make honey. Such inborn longings don't merit praise or blame.

"In order for your deepest longing and all your other loves to fit together, you are born with a free will which advises you and ought to guard the doorway of your decisions. According to how well this part of you separates good loves from evil loves, you come to merit praise or blame. Those thinkers who reasoned far enough perceived free will and gave the world its moral codes. Suppose, if you like, that every love you feel comes to you unbidden; you still have the power to refuse it. Beatrice understands that this noble power is free will; keep it in mind in case she speaks to you about it."[1]

The moon hadn't come up until almost midnight, and it made the stars seem to fade. It looked like a bucket as bright as fire, and it crossed the path the sun travels when Romans watch it on its way from Sardinia to sunset in Corsica. Now the noble one who had made Pietola the most famous town in Mantua had completed the task I

---

[1] Dorothy Sayers points out that two freedoms are involved: freedom of choice and power to implement the choice. When judgment is enslaved, one cannot choose what is right. When will is enslaved, one cannot do what one judges right. Beatrice will show Dante how God frees a person to do what he chooses to do.

set him.[2] At that point, like one who received good answers to his questions, I relaxed and let my mind ramble drowsily.

All at once I was jolted out of my dreaminess by people who had approached us from behind. Just as the Ismenus and Asopus rivers used to see a mad rush along their banks at night when the people of Thebes called upon Bacchus,[3] so around the ledge I saw a throng rushing toward us faster and faster, as if good will and just love were spurring them on. Because they were all running they were soon upon us, and the two in front were shouting with tears: "Mary ran to the hills with haste,"[4] and "When he subdued Ilerda, Caesar stabbed Marseilles and raced on into Spain."[5]

Those who followed cried, "Hurry! Hurry! Don't lose precious time by loving too little. Strive harder to do well, for more grace!"[6]

"You zealous runners, who are perhaps trying to catch up after being slow to do good until now, this living man (and I am certainly not lying) wants to climb higher when the sun shines on us again; so tell us where the nearest opening is."

---

[2]Virgil was born in Pietola.

[3]Throngs with torches would run along the river banks at night to appeal to Bacchus for rain for their vineyards.

[4]Luke 1:39.

[5]Caesar left Brutus at Marseilles and rushed on to attack Pompey's generals in Spain.

[6]The sin of sloth takes many forms. Dorothy Sayers points out that it is not only idleness of mind and laziness of body, but also an attitude of indifference that extends to a deliberate refusal of joy and even self-induced despair. The form of sloth called "tolerance" acquiesces to evil and error. The form of sloth called "disillusionment" rejects what is good and beautiful. The form of sloth called "escapism" is a withdrawal into isolation. The spiritual antidote to sloth is active zeal. No verbal prayer is provided on the ledge of the slothful, because for them "to labor is to pray."

My Teacher said that, and a spirit answered: "Follow us, and you'll find the passageway. We can't stop, because we are in such a rush; therefore forgive us if our penance seems rude. I was the Abbot of San Zeno at Verona under the good Barbarossa, whom Milan speaks of with tears. And I know someone who has a foot in the grave already who will soon repent for ruling the monastery there, because in place of its true pastor he has put his son in charge, a man conceived in shame and deformed in body and mind."[7] I don't know if he said more or was silent, because by now he had raced on; but I heard that much and chose to remember it.

The one who was my help in every need said, "Turn this way and look at two more who come along crying against sloth." The last two shouted: "The people for whom the sea opened were dead before Jordan saw their heirs,"[8] and "Those folks who did not work to the end for Anchises' son lived on in shame."[9]

When those spirits were out of sight, a new thought came to mind, and then many others; and so I drifted from one to another and on into dream.

---

[7] Alberto della Scala was the father of Dante's good friends Bartolommeo and Cam Grande. Alberto died in 1301, ten years after appointing his depraved son Giuseppe to be the abbot. Giuseppe held that post from 1291 to 1314, and Dante visited Verona from 1303 to 1304; so the two may have been acquainted. Dante's friends evidently loathed their half-brother, judging from Dante's description of him.

[8] According to Exodus, Numbers, and Deuteronomy, the generation of Hebrews who escaped from Egypt across the Red Sea all died before reaching the promised land, due to their complaining and lack of loyalty to Moses.

[9] According to Virgil's *Aeneid,* some of the wandering Trojans settled in Sicily rather than following Aeneus all the way to Italy.

CANTO NINETEEN

Sweet Song of the Siren

At that hour when the heat of the previous day no longer lingers on the cold earth to counterbalance the chilly light of the moon or Saturn,[1] when the geomancers see their Fortuna Major[2] rising in the east before dawn, when little darkness is left—at that hour I had a dream.[3] I was approached by a stuttering, squint-eyed woman with club feet, crippled hands, and bleached-out skin.

I looked at her; and just as the morning sun warms arms and legs that are stiff with cold, my gaze loosened her tongue, and soon all of her was whole and straight, and her pale face became colorful, as love would wish it. When her tongue was thus set loose she began to sing, so that it would have been difficult to wrench away my attention.[4]

---

[1]Saturn, being far from the sun, was considered frigid; and so was the moon.

[2]Geomancers predicted events according to certain patterns of earth they cast onto the ground or patterns of dots, and they called one of the patterns Fortuna Major.

[3]It has been observed since antiquity that rapid-eye-movement dreams late in the nightly sleep cycle are most apt to be significant and to convey truth.

[4]Dorothy Sayers explains that in this complex and profound dream the siren is Lilith, the legendary first wife of Adam, who was only a magical image created by the Evil One. (In contrast, God created a real woman, Eve, to be loved and respected by Adam.) Dante's siren acquired the appearance of strength and beauty from his attention to

"I am the sweet siren," she sang. "I am the one who leads sailors astray at sea, such pleasures are in my songs. I lured Ulysses from his wandering way with my music, and those who live with me rarely depart, they are so well satisfied."

Her mouth was not yet closed when a holy, alert lady appeared beside me to oppose her. "O Virgil, Virgil, who is this?" she demanded, and he approached with his eyes fixed upon her. He seized the other woman and ripped her clothes, exposing the front of her body and showing me her belly. The stench of her body awakened me.[5]

I turned my eyes to Virgil, and he said, "I've called you at least three times. Rise and come with me to find the opening where we may enter."

I lifted myself up, and all the circles of the holy mountain were filled now with daylight, and we walked with the sun on our backs. Following Virgil, with my crooked brow resembling a man so burdened with thought that his back is bent like half an arched bridge, I heard the words "Come, here's the pass" pronounced in a tone more gentle and kind than is ever heard on earth.

With outspread wings like those of a swan, the speaker guided us up between two walls of solid stone. He fluttered his pinions then and fanned us, telling us that those who mourn are blessed, for they shall be richly comforted.[6]

---

her; thus she symbolizes a projection of his own desires, no more than an egotistical fantasy. She lures people into the sins of Upper Purgatory.

[5]According to Dorothy Sayers, the alert lady in Dante's dream probably stands for his own intuitive response to danger, and Virgil stands for reason. Charles Williams' novel *Descent into Hell* is an imaginative expansion and interpretation of Dante's dream of the siren.

It sometimes happens that a sleeper is awakened by a symbolic event in a dream when a related event is actually occurring in real life.

[6]Matthew 5:4. The Angel of Zeal has erased the fourth P from Dante's forehead.

"What ails you?" my Teacher began to ask me, "that you keep staring at the ground?" (We had moved on up from the angel.)

I said, "I'm terrified by a strange dream I can't get out of my mind."

"Have you seen," he asked, "that ancient witch who has caused the spirits up ahead of us to weep? Did you see how people can get free from her? Let that be enough. Scorn the earth beneath your feet and turn your eyes instead to the lure that the eternal King whirls around the skies."[7]

As a falcon gazes at its feet, then turns when called and spreads its wings with eagerness for food, so I responded. So I climbed up the rest of the rocky passage to the next ledge. Once I was out onto the fifth circle, I saw spirits scattered about weeping, face downward on the ground.[8]

"My soul cleaves to the dust," they said, with such groans that one could hardly understand their words.[9]

"Spirits chosen by God, whose sufferings help you toward both justice and hope, point us toward the upward path."

"If you are not forced to lie here on your face, and want to find the path quickly, keep the rim of the ledge to your right."

Thus the poet made his request and an answer came in front of us, and I noticed what was contained in those

---

[7]Dante likens the way God lures a person higher to the way a handler of falcons lures it into the air by slinging up a small feathered decoy to attract it.

[8]These are the covetous, who had an inordinate love of wealth, and the status and power that wealth confers. Because they have focused upon things of this earth, they can see nothing but the earth until they are cured.

[9]Psalm 119:25.

words.[10] I looked toward my lord, and he signaled agreement to what my look was asking for. Once I had that permission, I approached the creature whose words had so impressed me, saying, "Spirit, in whom weeping nurtures what is needed for turning to God, put aside your burden for me. Tell me who you were and why your back is upward—and tell me if you want anything from me when I, a living man, return where I have come from."

He answered, "You will learn why heaven turns our backs toward heaven, but first you must know that I was Pope. Between Sesti and Chiaveri a fair river flows down, and my family got its title there. In a little over one month[11] I learned that one who keeps the cloak out of the mud finds it so heavy that all other burdens seem as light as feathers. My conversion—alas!—was belated, but when I became Pastor of Rome I discovered how false life is. I saw that the heart has no rest there, nor could one rise any higher; therefore I began to value heaven. Until then, I had been a wretched soul, apart from God, entirely greedy; and now, as you see, I am paying for that.

"The result of greed is evident here in the cleansing of the turned-down souls, and there is no more bitter penalty in purgatory. Even as our eyes were fixed on earthly things and did not look toward heaven, so justice forces our eyes to the earth. As greed spoiled our love for what was good and kept us from good works, so justice binds our hands and feet and holds us fast. And so long as it pleases God, we will lie here stretched out motionless."

---

[10]Dorothy Sayers points out that until now Dante has not considered the idea that the spirits consigned to Purgatory may pass freely through any circles where they have no personal need for cleansing.

[11] Adrian V was Pope for only 38 days.

I had knelt down and was going to speak, but as I began he could tell where I was by my voice. "Why have you knelt down here?"

"Because my conscience won't let me stand in the presence of your dignity."

"Straighten up, my brother," he said. "Mistake it not, I am a fellow-servant of the one Ruler, with you and with others. If you ever understood the holy gospel message 'They neither marry...', you can see why I say this.[12] Now go along; I don't want you to stay longer because your lingering interrupts my weeping, by which I nurture what you said I do.

"I have a niece over there named Alagia, a good woman so long as she doesn't become evil by following the family example; and she is the only one I have left there."[13]

---

[12] Christ answered the Sadducees in Matthew 22:23-30, Mark 12:18-25, and Luke 22:27-35 by stating that people neither marry nor are given in marriage in heaven. All such earthly ties and titles are dissolved in heaven, including the papacy.

[13] According to John Ciardi, Dante had been well treated by Alagia's husband Moroello Malaspina and admired Alagia for her good works.

CANTO TWENTY

The Great Earthquake

It's useless to struggle against a stronger will; therefore, against my pleasure, to please him, I withdrew my sponge from the water when it was still half dry.[1] I moved on with my Guide where we found space near the rocky mountainside, as one walking on a castle wall stays close to the battlements; because those who were distilling the sin of the world through their eyes, drop by drop, clustered near the edge.

Damn you for your bottomless craving, you ancient she-wolf that consumes more prey than any other beast![2] You, heavens, whose turnings supposedly change conditions down on the earth, when will the one come who will drive her away?

We went on a few slow steps farther, and I was fully absorbed in the souls I heard pitifully weeping and sorrowing. By chance I heard one in front of us call out "Sweet Mary" like a woman in pain of childbirth; and the voice went on, "How poor you were we know from the inn where you lay down your holy burden."[3]

---

[1] Dante withdrew the sponge of his curiosity from the water of Adrian's knowledge although he was not yet satisfied.

[2] The wolf is covetousness. Dorothy Sayers points out that worldly ambition is accompanied by covetousness for wealth and possessions, "with the inevitable manifestations of cruelty, callousness, and meanness, as exemplified in the history of the House of Capet."

[3] Luke 2:7.

Next I heard, "Good Fabricus, you chose to possess virtue with poverty, rather than wealth with vice."[4] These words were so pleasant that I hurried forward to learn from the spirit who seemed to have said them. It went on speaking about the treasure that Nicholas gave to the maidens to insure their virtue.[5]

"Spirit who speaks so much about good, tell me who you were," I said, "and why you alone praise these good deeds. Your answer will not go unrewarded, if I return to complete my fleeting life."

He answered, "I will tell you, not for any comfort I expect from over there, but because so much grace shines in you before you are dead. I was the root of the evil tree that shades all Christian lands, so that little good fruit is harvested there. But if Douay, Lille, Ghent and Bruges were powerful enough, they would take vengeance upon it, and I pray for that.[6] Over there I was called Hugh Capet, father of the Philips and Louises who have recently ruled France. My father was a Paris butcher. When the ancient line of kings ended, save for the one who donned a monk's gray robe, I found my hands grasping the reins of government of the realm—so powerful in possessions and

---

[4]Caius Fabricus was a Roman Consul who refused bribes and lived simply three centuries before the time of Christ.

[5]St. Nicholas secretly threw bags of gold into the home of an impoverished man to provide a dowry so that his three daughters could marry.

[6]The four chief cities of Flanders suffered abuse from the French, particularly in 1299 when Charles of Valois offered liberal terms of surrender to the honorable Count Guy of Flanders and then shamelessly betrayed his trust. In 1302 the Flemings got their revenge at the Battle of Courtrai, where they slaughtered the flower of French chivalry and 6,000 horses.

rich in friends that to the crown of France my son's head arose, and from him issued all those royal bones.[7]

"So long as the great dowry of Provence had not deprived my progeny of any sense of decency, they were neither very good nor very bad.[8] Then by force and fraud their rapacity began; and afterward, to make amends, they seized Normandy, Ponthieu, and Gascony. To make amends, Charles came to Italy, victimized Conradin, and sent Thomas on to heaven—to make amends.[9]

"I see a day coming soon that brings another Charles out of France to make himself and his family famous. He comes alone, unarmed except for the spear that Judas used, and thrusts it so hard that it bursts the guts of Florence. He wins no land, just sin and shame; but to make them even worse, he takes them lightly.[10]

"Yet another Charles I see, once captive in a ship, selling his daughter and haggling over the price like a

---

[7]Hugh Capet the Great died in 987, and his son Hugh Capet ruled France from 987 to 996. Dante seems to have combined the two. Dante portrays Hugh Capet in Purgatory condemning the dishonorable role of his progeny three centuries after his death and just two years before some of their victims are avenged. In the Capetian dynasty there were eight kings named Philip or Louis.

[8]In the middle of the thirteenth century Louis IX and his brother Charles of Anjou married two daughters of the late Count of Provence, Margaret and Beatrice, and laid claim to the land as their dowry.

[9]Charles of Anjou attacked Manfred at the Battle of Benevento in 1266, and had 17-year-old Conradin beheaded after defeating him in 1268. It was rumored that he had Thomas Aquinas poisoned. (Note the heavy irony in Dante's phrase "to make amends.")

[10]Charles of Valois intervened in the political turmoil in Florence in 1301, allegedly as an even-handed peacemaker. Instead, he turned Florence over to the Black party, which banished all the Whites—including Dante.

pirate selling slavegirls.[11] Avarice, what more can you do to us after seducing my family so that it willingly betrays its own flesh and blood?

"As if to make future and past evils seem less, I see Philip the Fair enter Alagna and capture the vicar of Christ. I see Christ mocked again, the gall and vinegar returned, and death this time between two living thieves. I see the new Pilate so cruel that this is not enough, and so he sails greedily into the temple.[12]

"God, when shall I rejoice to see the vengeance which invisibly sweetens your anger in your secret will?[13]

"What I was saying about the only Bride of the Holy Spirit, which made you turn to me for explanation, such is the summation of all our daytime prayers.[14] But when night falls, we speak the opposite instead. Then we tell of Pygmalion, whose lust for gold made him turn traitor,

---

[11]Charles II of Anjou, son of Charles I of Anjou, was the father of Dante's friend Charles Martel. He accepted money from disreputable old Azzo d'Este in return for his daughter's hand in marriage.

[12]In 1303 Philip mounted charges of heresy and misconduct against the notorious 86-year-old Pope Boniface VII, who decided to excommunicate Philip in response. Acting for Philip, Sciarra di Colonna and William de Nogaret broke in upon the Pope and held him prisoner for three days, mocking him and plundering his palace. As Christ died between two dying thieves, Boniface suffered between his captors, two living thieves—and died a few weeks later from the shock. Philip later caused Pope Clement V to persecute the Order of the Templars, ostensibly for heresy, but perhaps really for their treasures. Dorothy Sayers praises Dante's paradoxical and magnificently fair condemnation of those who attacked Pope Boniface, in spite of the fact that Boniface was an extremely evil man and Dante's most hated personal and political enemy. She calls this "a triumph of the passionate intellect..."

[13]Dorothy Sayers notes, "God's wrath, being pure of fear or passion or impatience, is without the haste, bitterness, and violence which we associate with human anger."

[14]Hugh Capet spoke about Mary and others who were not avaricious when Dante first noticed him.

thief, and killer of close kin; and the misery of miserly Midas, whose greedy request made him a joke forever. We remember reckless Achan, who stole some booty and seems to suffer still from Joshua's wrath. We condemn Sapphira and her husband, we praise the hooves that crushed Heliodorus, and all around this mountain Polymnestor, who killed Polydorus, resounds in infamy. Finally, we cry, 'Crassus, tell us, because you know, how does gold taste?'[15]

"Sometimes we speak, one loudly and another softly, according to our impulses, with great force or with little force. So I was not alone earlier in citing the good that we tell of in daytime, but no one near me happened to be raising his voice."

By then we had left him behind in our effort to advance as far as possible, when I felt the mountain quake as if it were collapsing; a chill seized me as it seizes someone who is dying. Surely Delos was not shaken so violently before Latona made her nest there to give birth to the sky's two eyes.[16]

---

[15]In *The Aeneid*, Pygmalion killed his brother-in-law for gold. In classical mythology, Midas wished that everything he touched would turn to gold, which made his food uneatable. In the book of Joshua in the Old Testament, Achan was executed for stealing part of the captured treasure that Joshua had consecrated to God. In the book of Acts in the New Testament, Ananias and Saphira were struck dead for falsely claiming to put all they had into communal living. In the book of 2 Maccabees in the Old Testament Apocrypha, Heliodorus tried to commit armed robbery of the temple in Jerusalem and was killed by a supernatural horse and rider. In *The Aeneid* King Polymnestor killed his son for some Trojan gold. In classical history, Crassus "the Rich" was a partner of Caesar and Pompey; he was killed in battle against the Parthians, whose king knew of his greed and had molten gold poured down his throat.

[16]In one account in Greek mythology, Jupiter caused a huge earthquake to raise the island of Delos before Latona came there to give birth to the twins Apollo (the sun) and Diana (the moon).

Then a shout arose around us, so that my Teacher drew me close and said, "Don't be afraid, so long as I'm your Guide."

"Gloria in excelsis Deo" they cried, judging from what I heard from those near by. We stood alertly motionless, like the shepherds who first heard that hymn, until the quaking stopped and the song ended.[17] Then we started on our way again, looking at the souls on the ground who were back at their weeping. If my memory serves me right, no ignorance had ever so tormented me with thirst for knowledge as I pondered; but in our rush I was not bold enough to ask. By myself, I could make nothing of it; and so I continued, timid and pensive.

---

[17]"Glory to God in the highest" is what shepherds out in the field heard the angels sing when Christ was born, recorded in Luke 2:8-14.

CANTO TWENTY-ONE

Meeting an Admirer

The natural thirst which is never quenched[1] except by the water asked for by the poor woman of Samaria[2] was burning in me, and haste was rushing me along the difficult path behind my Guide, and I was full of pity for the just vengeance; and then, just as Luke tells us that Christ—already risen from the tomb—appeared to the two on the road,[3] so a soul overtook us; and because our eyes were on the sufferers on the ground we were oblivious to him until he said, "My brothers, God's peace to you."

We turned quickly, and Virgil responded with the appropriate sign.[4] Then he said, "May the just court that doomed me to eternal exile bring you in peace to the blessed gathering."

As we continued forward, the newcomer asked, "If you are souls that God does not allow above, who has brought you this far up his stairs?"

My teacher answered, "If you look at the marks on this man's face, put there by the angel, you will see that he is fit to rule with the good. But since she who spins day and

---

[1]Dante refers to Aristotle's statement "All men naturally desire knowledge."

[2]John 4:7-15. Christ said to the Samaritan woman he met at the well, "Whoever drinks of the water that I give her will never thirst..."

[3]Luke 24:13-15. As two disciples walked along the road to Emmaus, Christ was suddenly walking along with them.

[4]The traditional response was "And to your spirit."

night has not yet finished his length of thread, which Clotho winds on her skein for each person,[5] his spirit, a sister to yours and mine, could not come here alone because it can't see as we can. Therefore I was brought out of the great jaws of Hell to guide him, and I will guide him on as far as my knowledge enables me to go.

"But tell us, if you know, why the mountain shook so and why everyone seemed to cry out in unison down to the muddy seaside." By asking this, he threaded the needle's eye of my desire, and hope for an answer made my thirst less severe.

The spirit began, "On this mountain, sacred order allows nothing irregular or uncustomary. It is free from earthly variability. What Heaven takes back into itself from here[6] is directed by its true self and nothing else, because neither rain nor hail nor snow nor dew nor hoarfrost falls above the short little stairway of three steps. There are no clouds, thick or thin, nor lightning flash, nor sign of Thaumas's daughter who often moves about.[7] Weather rises no higher than the top of the three steps I mentioned, where Peter's vicar has his feet.[8]

"Below that point perhaps the mountain quakes more or less, but up here no hidden underground wind (I don't know how it is) has ever caused a tremor.[9] This mountain quakes whenever some soul feels cleansed and ready to get up and move on higher, and then loud rejoicing is heard. The choice is the proof of the cleansing; desire fills

---

[5] In classical mythology the three Fates controlled individual human destiny: Lachesis spun the thread of life, Clotho wound it, and Atropos cut it off.

[6] Human souls in Purgatory are no longer influenced by inner or outer weather.

[7] In classical mythology, Thaumas's daughter was the rainbow.

[8] According to Dorothy Sayers, Peter's Gate is so high that there is no atmosphere above it. (The mountain is over 3,000 miles high.)

[9] Aristotle taught that underground winds caused earthquakes.

the soul and suddenly enables it to move on. That soul had the desire to ascend before, but the counter-desire for penance overruled it, as sin used to do.

"I lay under this torment for over five-hundred years, and only now felt my will set free for a higher threshold. Therefore you felt the shock and heard the reverent spirits around the mountain give praise to God—may He soon send them above." Thus he spoke to us, and since we relish a drink according to how thirsty we were, I can't tell you how much good he did me.[10]

My wise guide said, "Now I understand the net that holds you here and how one breaks free, and the earthquake, and you have made me glad. Now please tell me who you were; and in your own words why you have lain here such long ages."

"Back in the days when good Titus, with the Highest King's help, avenged the wounds that shed the blood betrayed by Judas,[11] I had the most enduring and honorable title—with much fame but without faith. Over there the music of my words was so sweet that I was called from Toulouse to Rome and crowned with myrtle.[12]

"People over there still remember Statius.[13] I wrote about Thebes, and then about the great Achilles; but I

---

[10]Statius is a companion to Dante from here to Paradise.

[11]In 70 A.D. Titus besieged and captured Jerusalem. He served as Emperor in 79-81 A.D. and was much loved by the Romans for his kindness.

[12]The spirit indicates that he was a famous poet. It was thought in Dante's day that he was from Toulouse; but in fact he was from Naples.

[13]Publius Papinius Statius (circa 45-96 A.D.) was a popular poet in his own day and in Dante's day. His surviving poetry does not mention a conversion to Christianity, but C. S. Lewis believed that Dante had good grounds for believing or inventing such a conversion. In his 1936 study of medieval literature, *The Allegory of Love,* C. S. Lewis perceived in the poetry of Statius the earliest use of allegory as a literary form, which would be one reason for Dante's great interest in him. In his 1957

died working on the latter. The sparks that warmed me and ignited my poetic fire were from the divine flame that has kindled more than a thousand poets: *The Aeneid*, which was both mother and nurse to me. Without it my work would not have weighed an ounce. If I could have lived over there when Virgil was alive, I would agree to an extra year of exile in Purgatory."

At those words Virgil shot me a glance that signaled "Silence." But good intentions are not all powerful, because laughter and tears are so quickly triggered that they are often disobedient. I did no more than smile, but the spirit fell silent and stared into my eyes, where the truth shows.

"May your efforts achieve your goal," he said. "Why did your face just now flicker with suppressed laughter?" At that, I'm caught on both sides; one bids me be silent and the other bids me speak.

I sighed, and my teacher understood and said, "Go ahead and speak, and tell him what he asks for so earnestly."

Therefore I said, "Perhaps you were surprised by my smile, spirit of old, but here is a greater surprise for you by far. This one who guides my eyes upward is the same Virgil from whom you got the power to write poetry about men and gods. If you thought of any other reason for my laughter, set it aside as untrue and believe it was only your words about him."

---

essay "Dante's Statius," available in *Studies in Medieval and Renaissance Literature* (Cambridge University Press, 1966), Lewis notes that every major character in Statius's *Thebaid* is mentioned in Dante's *Comedy*. Statius will accompany Dante and Virgil through the rest of their sojourn in Purgatory.

He was already kneeling to kiss my teacher's feet, but Virgil said, "Brother, don't do that, because you are a spirit and so am I."[14]

And Statius said, rising, "Now you can see how much love for you warms me, when I forget our nothingness and treat these shadows like material things."

---

[14]When the poet Sordello knelt to kiss Virgil's feet below Peter's Gate (Cantos 7-9), Virgil did not object, and it seemed appropriate. But when Dante knelt to honor Pope Adrian on the fifth ledge (Canto 19), Adrian explained that he must not do so because they were fellow-servants of God. Now Virgil also refuses such earthly honor.

CANTO TWENTY-TWO

A Fragrant Fruit Tree

The angel had already come and gone, pointing us toward the sixth circle after erasing one more scar from my face. He told us that those who thirst for righteousness are blessed. (He included thirst and nothing else.)[1]

I felt lighter than I had on the previous climbs, and I was following the swift spirits upward effortlessly when Virgil began: "Love, set aflame by virtue, ignites corresponding love if its fire is seen. Ever since Juvenal descended into Limbo and told me of your high regard for me,[2] my good will toward you has exceeded what I've felt for anyone else I had not yet met. Therefore, these stairs we climb will seem short to me.

"Tell me, and forgive me as a friend if I'm presumptuous, and tell me so as a friend: how could financial greed find a place in your heart when you had carefully filled yourself with so much wisdom?"

These words caused Statius to chuckle wryly; then he answered: "Every word of yours is a precious sign of your love to me. Yes, things often seem contradictory when they are not, because the reasons for them are hidden. Your

---

[1] The angel of liberality has erased the fifth P from Dante's forehead, the mark of the sin of avarice. Matthew 5:6. The part of the beatitude about hungering for righteousness is reserved for the next angel, on the sixth ledge. Ledge five removed the stain of avarice, and ledge six will remove the stain of gluttony.

[2] Juvenal was a Roman poet and satirist who lived from approximately 47 to 130 A.D. and admired the writings of Statius.

question shows me that you think I was a miser in that other life, perhaps because of the circle where I stayed. Now I realize that miserliness was all too foreign to me, and for this flaw thousands of months have punished my excess.

"And if I had not reformed when I took seriously your lines where you rage against human nature 'Why don't you limit the lust of mortals, you sacred greed for gold?'[3] — I would be rolling weights in Hell's jousts.[4] I realized then that our hands could spread their wings too wide in spending, and I repented that and other sins. How many bald prodigals will go to their judgment because they failed to repent in or at the end of life due to ignorance! And know that the fault which counteracts a sin with its direct opposite here, added to it, withers the sin. Therefore if I was here among the wailing misers to be cleansed, this happened to me because I was the opposite."

"Now, when you wrote about the savage wars of Jocasta's two-fold sorrow,"[5] said the writer of the Bucolic

---

[3] This loose quotation is from Virgil's *Aeneid*, Book 3, lines 56-57.

[4] In Canto 7 of *The Inferno*, hoarders and wasters roll great weights at each other.

[5] Jocasta's twin sons Eteocles and Polynices were also her grandsons, because as a widow she had unwittingly married her long-lost son Oedipus. The twins initially agreed to share the throne of Thebes, but went to war over it and finally killed each other, as Statius recounted in his epic *Thebaid*.

If they ever really existed, the legendary Oedipus and his doomed family lived in Thebes, northwest of Athens, perhaps 3500 years ago and 1000 years before the Greek dramatist Sophocles immortalized them in his tragedies. Almost 500 years later, Statius wrote about the family in Latin. Almost 1300 years later, Dante wrote in Italian about Statius writing about it in Latin. Finally, another 600 years later, Sigmund Freud wrote about the family in German and invented the misleading term "Oedipus complex." On November 11, 1955, Dorothy Sayers responded at the Royal Institution of England with her

poems,[6] "judging from what you and Clio tell there,[7] it does not seem that faith had yet made you faithful; and without faith good works are not enough. If this is the case, what sun or candlelight cast back the darkness for you, so that you set your sails to follow the Fisherman?"[8]

Statius answered, "You first sent me to Parnasus to drink in its caves,[9] and then lit my way to God. You did that like one who walks at night with his light behind him to guide others, not himself, when you said, 'A great order of the ages is born anew. Now the virgin, now the reign of Saturn, comes again; now a new progeny descends from heaven.'[10]

"Through you I became a poet, and through you a Christian; but so that you may see more fully what I outline thus, I'll fill in the color. The world was already pregnant with the true faith, disseminated by the messengers of the Everlasting Kingdom; and your words, that I just mentioned, harmonized so well with the new

---

profoundly witty address "Oedipus Simplex," published in 1963 in the collection *The Poetry of Search and the Poetry of Statement* (London: Victor Gollancz Ltd.).

[6]Virgil wrote bucolic poems called *Eclogues*, and Statius is about to quote from one

[7]Clio, the muse of history, was invoked by Statius when he wrote *Thebaid*.

[8]Matthew 4:18-20 (NIV), "As Jesus was walking beside the Sea of Galilee, he saw two brothers, Simon called Peter and his brother Andrew. They were casting a net into the lake, for they were fishermen. 'Come, follow me,' Jesus said, 'and I will make you fishers of men.' At once they left their nets and followed him."

[9]In classical mythology, Apollo and the muses had a sacred cave and sacred spring on Mount Parnasus. Statius means that Virgil inspired him to be a poet.

[10]Virgil's Fourth Eclogue, written shortly before the birth of Christ, has often been interpreted as a prophecy of that event. (Therefore John Dryden's translation of the Fourth Eclogue is quoted in Handel's *Messiah*.)

preachers that I often visited them. They became so saintly in my sight that when Domitian persecuted them, their cries were all accompanied by my tears.[11]

"When I was walking in that world, I helped them, and their holy lives made me scorn all other sects. Before I had brought the Greeks to the rivers of Thebes in my poem, I was baptized; but because of fear I remained a secret Christian, long pretending to be a pagan. That lukewarmness later forced me to rush around the fourth ledge for more than four centuries.

"You, therefore, who lifted the veil for me that had hid the great good I describe, while we have free time during this climb, tell me where is our ancient Terrence, and Caecilus, Plautus and Varro if you know.[12] Tell me if they are damned, and in which section."

"They and Persius and I and many others," my leader answered, "are with that Greek to whom the muses gave more milk than any other,[13] in the first circle of the dark prison. We often talk of the mount where those wetnurses dwell.[14] Euripides is there with us, Antithon, Simonides, Agathon, and many other Greeks who wore laurel on their brows.[15] There one can see—of your people—Antigone, Deiphyle, Argia, and Ismene, still as sad as she was. There one can see the woman who showed the Langlia, and there Tiresias's daughter. There Thetis, and Deidamia with her sisters."[16]

---

[11]The Roman Emperor Domitian (81-96 A.D.) allegedly persecuted Christians. He sponsored poverty-stricken Statius, who honored him lavishly for it in *Thebaid*.

[12]These were all Roman dramatists and poets.

[13]Homer was given more inspired talent than any other poet.

[14]In limbo, dead authors talk wistfully about the art they loved.

[15]These were all Greek dramatists and poets.

[16]These are all people Statius wrote about.

Both poets became silent, newly intent on gazing around now that they were out of the walled stairway. Four handmaidens of the day were retired and the fifth was in charge now, steering the flaming chariot higher.[17] My leader said, "I think we should keep our right shoulders toward the rim and circle the mountain in our usual way."

So custom was our guide, and we went on our way with little misgiving because of the agreement of the pure soul.[18] They traveled on in front and I came alone behind; and I listened to their discussion, which taught me much about poetry. But soon the pleasant talk was interrupted by a tree that we discovered in the road. It had beautiful, fragrant fruit.

Just as a pine tree narrows upward from bough to bough, so this one narrowed downward; I think so that no one could climb it. And from the rock wall at the side, a clear waterfall showered the leaves with spray. The two poets approached the tree, and a voice from within the foliage cried, "This food shall famish you."[19]

Then it continued, "Mary cared more about making the wedding feast full and proper than about her own mouth, which now prays for you.[20]

"Long ago, Roman women were content to drink water;[21] and Daniel rejected food and gained wisdom.[22]

---

[17] The first four hours of the day are past, which means that it is now past 10 a.m. The friends have been on the sixth ledge for four hours, and the chariot of the sun is high.

[18] Statius was a pure soul because he was ready now to enter heaven

[19] The sixth ledge is the one where the stain of gluttony is washed away.

[20] The story of Mary at the wedding in Cana is told in John 2: 1-12.

[21] It has been claimed that in the early days Roman women drank no wine.

[22] As recounted in the first chapter of *Daniel*, this valuable Hebrew captive in the royal court in Babylon faithfully insisted upon vegetables

"The first age was golden; then acorns tasted good and every stream tasted like nectar.[23]

"Locusts and honey were the food that nourished the Baptist in the wilderness; therefore he has glory as great as the Gospel tells you."[24]

---

and water instead of the royal diet that he was expected to eat; and he became healthier and stronger looking than those who ate luxurious food.

[23]Ovid told about a fabulous golden age in the early history of the human race.

[24]The living conditions of John the Baptist in the wilderness are described in Matthew 3:1-6 and Mark 1:4-8.

CANTO TWENTY-THREE

Singing through Tears

As I gazed at the green leaves like one who wastes his life stalking little birds, my more-than-father said to me, "Son, come along now, for we must use the time allotted us more wisely than this." I turned my face and my steps just as promptly, to follow the two sages—whose talk made the going easy.

And suddenly in tears and song "O Lord, open my lips" was heard, causing both joy and pain.[1]

"Dearest father, what do I hear?" I asked, and he answered, "Spirits who are probably loosening the knot of debt that binds them."

Just as preoccupied travelers who overtake strangers on the road will glance at them as they pass, so a crowd of silent and devout souls came from behind us and hurried by, glancing at us as they passed. Each of them was darkly hollow-eyed and pale-faced, and so emaciated that the skin clung to the bones. I don't think that Erisichthon was ever this dried up into a mere hide, even when his fear of starving was worst.[2] I thought to myself,

---

[1] Psalm 51:15 consists of the plea "O Lord, open my lips. and my mouth will declare your praise." Sung in Latin, the opening phrase was "*Labia mea, Domine.*" This is the prayer of reformed gluttons, because the mouth was made for more than eating and drinking (symbols of consumption). Dorothy Sayers points out that gluttony takes many forms and can consist of an uncontrolled appetite for quality rather than quantity.

[2] In classical mythology Erisichthon chopped down an oak in a grove sacred to the goddess Ceres and was condemned to insatiable

"I see here the people who lost Jerusalem when Miriam ripped her son with her beak."[3]

The sockets of their eyes seemed like rings with the gems missing. Anyone who reads the letters OMO in a human face would see the M clearly.[4] Who would think, if he didn't know the reason, that the scent of fruit and water could create craving that could do this to people?

I was still wondering what had famished them, because the reason for their emaciation and flaky skin was not yet clear, when suddenly a spirit turned his deeply sunken eyes on me and stared, then shouted: "What grace is bestowed upon me!" I would never have recognized his face, but his voice showed me what his face did not. The spark rekindled in me my knowledge of his features, and I recognized the face of Forese.[5]

"Don't be distracted by the dry scabbiness that bleaches my skin," he begged, "nor by my missing flesh, but tell me the truth about yourself; and who those two

---

hunger that forced him to sell all his ancestral wealth and to repeatedly sell his daughter (who always returned in a different form). His hunger finally became so overpowering ("when his fear of starving was worst") that he devoured himself.

[3] According to the first-century historian Flavius Josephus, in the siege of Jerusalem by Titus in 70 A.D., a woman named Miriam killed her baby, roasted him, and ate him.

[4] The Latin word for a human is homo. Some medieval people used to liken human eyes to O's, and the bones that protect the eyes (the cheekbones, the brow ridge, and the nose) to a large uncial (roundly bulging) letter M, as if the human face bore a logo. Starvation would make the bone structure of the M far more prominent.

[5] Forese, who died on July 28, 1296, was a distant relative of Dante's wife and a good friend of Dante's until they were separated by politics. At one time the two had written a series of outrageously insulting and vulgar sonnets to each other, a popular custom rather like today's more or less friendly "roasts." In one of those sonnets Dante had accused Forese of gluttony, pride, and wastefulness.

spirits are that are your escorts. Don't hold back from speaking to me!"

"Your face," I answered, "which I once wept for in death, now grieves me to tears again, seeing it so ravaged. Therefore, in God's name tell me what has done this to you. Don't make me speak when I am so bewildered, for one speaks poorly when consumed with another matter."

He answered, "By divine providence, there is a power in the water and the tree we went past that makes me so thin. All these people who sob and sing, who were ruled by their appetites, are making themselves holy here in hunger and thirst. The fragrance which floats off the fruit, and off the spray that moistens the greenery, makes us crave food and drink. And not only once is this pain renewed as we keep circling this road.[6] I say pain, but I should say solace; for the same desire draws us to the tree which caused Christ to joyfully cry 'Eli' when he delivered us with his blood."[7]

I said to him, "Forese, since the day when you switched worlds for a better life, less than five years have passed so far. If your power to go on sinning ended before you repented—the holy sorrow that re-weds our souls to God—then how have you got up here? I expected to find you down below still, where one works off time."[8]

Upon that, he answered, "My Nella, with her flood of tears, has brought me this level quickly to drink the sweet

---

[6] As long as souls are at this level of purgatory, they keep circling past the fragrant tree that makes them starve afresh.

[7] See Matthew 27:46. At the ninth hour Jesus cried out in a loud voice, "*Eli, Eli, lama sabachthani*," meaning "My God, my God, why have you forsaken me!" As Christ joyfully suffered pain to save mankind, so these spirits joyfully suffer pain for the same reason: to conform to the will of God.

[8] Because Forese did not repent until he was on his deathbed, Dante wonders why he is not held outside the Gate with the Indolent for a term equal to his life on earth.

wormwood of my torment.[9] By her devout prayers and sighs she brought me from the border where one waits, and released me from the other circles.[10] And my poor widow whom I loved so well is all the more dear and precious to God in that she is lonely in her goodness; the Barbagia of Sardinia has more decent women than the 'Barbagia' where I left her.[11]

"I can foresee a future time not long from now when a decree from the pulpit will prohibit the brazen women of Florence from parading about with their bosoms bare to the nipples. What barbarian or Saracen women ever needed discipline to make them cover themselves? If these shameless ones knew what swift heaven was preparing for them, they would already have their mouths open to howl. If my foreknowledge is correct, they will be sad before sons now soothed with lullabies can grow beards on their cheeks.[12]

---

[9]Sweet wormwood is one of the paradoxes in this canto; how can bitterness be sweet? How can pain be joyful? How can a prayer be both sung and sobbed? How can the fragrance of food and drink make one emaciated?

[10]Forese has been speeded on his way up through Purgatory by his widow's fervent prayers. Just as we can bless people by praying for their spiritual welfare on earth, according to Dante we can bless them by praying for their spiritual welfare when they are on their way to Heaven.

[11]Ironically, Dante's crude sonnets to Forese (written years before Forese's death) included insults to Forese's wife Nella, along with embarrassing claims that Forese neglected her. By having the dead Forese praise the live Nella, Dante seems to have been apologizing to her. Nella lived in Florence, and Dante had Forese claim that there are more decent women in uncivilized Barbagia, with its bad reputation, than in Florence.

[12]Between 1301 and 1315 a series of military and natural disasters struck Florence.

"Now, brother, do not evade me any longer. You see that not only I but all these people are looking at where you cast a shadow."

I answered then, "If you recall what you have been with me and I have been with you, that memory will now be a grief.[13] I was turned away from that life by him who is leading me just the other day, when this one's (here I pointed at the sun) sister was full.[14] Through the deep night of the truly dead he has led me in this solid flesh that follows him. From there his encouragements have brought me upward, climbing and circling the mountain that makes you straight after the world has bent you. He says he will accompany me until I arrive where Beatrice is; there I must go on without him. It is Virgil who tells me this (I pointed to him); and this other is the soul for whom just now your realm, which is releasing him, shook every slope."

---

[13]Dante regrets the kind of life that he and Forese used to lead together in Florence.

[14]The moon is sometimes called the sister of the sun. (In classical mythology Diana, the moon, is sister of Apollo, the sun.) Dante refers to the fact that there was a full moon on the night of Holy Thursday when he was in the Dark Wood.

The Gluttons
Gustave Doré (Canto 24)

CANTO TWENTY-FOUR

The Beggars' Tree

Talking didn't slow our walking, and walking didn't slow our talking; while talking we moved on briskly like a ship driven by a good wind. And the souls, looking doubly dead, through their cavernous eyes drank in amazement at me, knowing I was alive.

Continuing my conversation with Forese, I said, "Perhaps he climbs more slowly than he would otherwise, because of his companion.[1] But tell me, if you can, where is Piccarda. And tell me if I can see anyone of significance among these staring at me."

"My sister—I don't know which was greater, her beauty or her goodness—triumphs now, crowned in joy on Mount Olympus."[2]

So he answered first, then added: "Here we are not forbidden to name everyone, since our facial features are sucked dry by total abstinence. This"—and he pointed with his finger—"is Bonagiunta, Bonagiunta of Lucca;[3] and that face beyond him, more emaciated than the rest, held the Holy Church in his arms. He came from Tours,

---

[1] Statius could have moved quickly on up to heaven, but he is taking advantage of this opportunity to talk with Virgil.

[2] Forese's sister Piccarda was a nun whose evil brother Corso forced her to break her vows and marry for his own political advancement. She has died and gone to Heaven—which Dante refers to here as Mount Olympus.

[3] Bonagiunta degli Overardi was an important poet and public speaker who died in 1297.

and by fasting he purges himself of eels from Bolsena and Vernaccia wine."[4]

He named many others to me, one by one, and all seemed glad to be named, so I saw not one dark look. I saw Ubaldino della Pila[5] and Boniface, who shepherded many people with his crook[6], both hungrily biting at thin air. I saw Messer Marchese, who used to drink leisurely at Forli because his thirst was never quenched, although he was never this thirsty there.[7]

But like one who glances around and then pays more attention to one person than to another, so I settled on the one from Lucca, who seemed most eager to meet me. He was muttering, and I heard something like "Gentucca" issue from the wound where Justice so emaciates them.[8]

"Soul," I said, "you who seem so eager to speak to me, speak so I can understand you, and give both of us some satisfaction."

"A woman is born and does not yet wear the marriage veil," he began, "who will make my city pleasant for you,

---

[4]Simon de Brie became Pope Martin IV (1281-1285). He was considered a good Pope, but reportedly such a glutton for eels boiled alive in sweet wine that he died from gorging on them. His face is probably the most emaciated because as Pope his gluttony was especially inappropriate.

[5]Ubaldino was a Ghibelline nobleman whose brother and son were encountered by Dante in *The Inferno*.

[6]This Boniface was the wealthy Archbishop of Ravenna (1274-1294). Instead of spiritually feeding and guiding the people in his archdiocese (with his shepherd's crook), he lavishly wined and dined political appointees and hangers-on.

[7]Marchese was known for drinking great quantities of wine, and laughingly justified it by saying he was always thirsty.

[8]Bonagiunta's wound is his dry, empty mouth, and he has apparently muttered the name of a housewife in Lucca who was kind to Dante in about 1308. But because this story is set in 1300, Gentucca would still be young and unmarried.

in spite of how some revile it.[9] You shall travel on with my prophecy; if you misunderstood my muttering, the actual events will make it clear to you.

"But tell me if I am looking at the man who created the new rhymes, one of which begins 'Ladies who have intelligence in love'."[10]

I answered, "I am one who, when Love inspires me, takes careful note; and in whatever style he dictates within me, I create."[11]

"Now I see, brother, the knot which held the Notary and Guittone and me back from the sweet new style I listen to.[12] I see clearly that your pens follow exactly the one who dictates, which was not the case with our pens. And no matter how hard one seeks, that is the only difference to be found between one style and another." As if satisfied, he fell silent.

As the birds that winter along the Nile sometimes flock in close formation, then speed off in single file — so everyone there sped away with swiftened pace, fleet because of leanness and desire. And as a weary runner lets his companions go on ahead and walks until the panting in his chest is eased, so Forese let the holy flock

---

[9]The demons in Canto 21 of *The Inferno* satirically reviled Lucca, the city of Saint Zita, for its graft.

[10]Bonagiuntahas quoted the first line of a poem in Dante's earlier *Vita Nuova*.

[11]Here Dante was paraphrasing a teaching of medieval mystics, that in order to speak fittingly of Love one must listen within one's heart and serve as a scribe.

[12]"The Notary "is 13th century poet Giacomo da Lentini, who represents the Sicilian school of love poetry. Guittone del Viva represents the old Tuscan school of love poetry. The superior "sweet new style" is that which originated with Guido Guinizelli, whom Dante refers to in Canto 26 as his poetic father. Because in real life Bonagiunta had attacked Guinizelli's style of love poetry, Dante has him admire it in Purgatory.

pass ahead and lagged behind with me, asking, "When shall I see you again?"

"I don't know how long I may live," I answered him, "but my return will not be soon enough to keep me from desiring to be already ashore; for the city where I was placed to live is day by day stripped of its goodness and seems doomed to dismal ruin."[13]

"Keep going," he said, "for I see the one who is most to blame for it dragged at a beast's tail toward the valley where sin is never washed away. The beast goes faster at every step, with ever increasing speed, until it smashes him and leaves his body hideously mangled. Those spheres don't have far to turn" (here he looked toward the sky) "before you see clearly what I cannot fully reveal.[14]

"Now you must stay behind, for time is precious in this realm, and I lose too much of it by traveling at your slow pace."

As a knight sometimes gallops away from his cavalry troop and wins the honor of striking the first blow in battle, so he parted from us with a lengthened stride; and I was left with only the two who were mighty directors of mankind. When he had pulled so far ahead of us that I could no more grasp him with my eyes than I could grasp what he said with my mind, I rounded the bend that led toward the green, heavy-laden boughs of another tree, not far away. I saw people beneath it lifting their hands and crying something at the leaves, like spoiled, greedy children who beg—when he from whom they beg won't

---

[13]Dante assures Forese that back on earth he will look forward to dying and arriving at the shore of Purgatory, because his beloved Florence keeps getting worse and worse.

[14]Forese is speaking of his own brother, Corso Donati, who was chiefly responsible for the massacre and expulsion of Dante's political party (the Whites) in 1301. Corso Donati got into trouble with his own party (the Blacks), and while trying to escape he was killed on October 6, 1308.

answer, but holds what they want in full view above them to tantalize them. Then they departed as if they were undeceived, and we arrived at the great tree which mocks so many prayers and tears.

"Pass onward without getting close to it; the tree from which Eve ate is higher up, and this tree is its offshoot."[15] I don't know who said this from the branches; therefore Virgil, Statius and I drew close together and edged along beside the rock wall.

"Remember," the voice said, "the cursed ones born of the clouds, with double chests, who gorged themselves and fought Theseus.[16] And the Hebrews who indulged themselves in drinking, so that Gideon rejected them when he went down the hills to Midian."[17] So we moved along close to the road's inner edge, hearing about rewards of sins of gluttony.

After we separated again, a thousand steps and more had brought us forward, each in silent contemplation. Suddenly a voice said, "Why are you three walking alone, lost in thought?" At that I was startled, like a timid, panicky animal.

I looked up to see who it was, and never in a furnace were red-hot glass or metal as bright as the face I saw. He said, "If you want to climb upward, here you must turn;

---

[15]In this story the Garden of Eden is a forest at the top of Mount Purgatory, and so the tree from which Eve ate is above the ledge devoted to cleansing souls from the stains of gluttony.

[16]The mythological centaurs were born to a cloud who took the form of a woman, and they were called double-breasted because they were half-horse, half-human. They drank too much wine at a wedding, tried to steal the bride, and were vanquished by Theseus.

[17]In Judges 7:5-6 Gideon followed God's instructions and dismissed his soldiers who quenched their thirst at the river by dipping their faces into the water rather than scooping up water in their hands in order to stay on guard. This selection process contributed to Gideon's victory.

for whoever travels to peace goes this way." His shining face blinded me, and so I followed the sounds of my teachers like one who finds his way with his ears.

Like the May breeze that stirs fragrantly and ushers in the dawn, laden with the sweetness of flowers and grass— so a wind brushed the middle of my forehead, and I clearly felt a soft wing that released ambrosial fragrance.[18]

I heard the words "Blessed are they who are so enlightened by grace that satisfaction does not kindle craving, and whose appetites are right."[19]

---

[18]The sixth P, the mark of the sin of gluttony, has been erased from Dante's forehead by the angel of temperance.

[19]Matthew 5:6 "Blessed are those who hunger and thirst after righteousness, for they shall be filled."

CANTO TWENTY-FIVE

Flames of Lust

Now it was time to climb without delay, for Taurus was at the sun's meridian, and Scorpio was at the night's.[1] Therefore, like a man who won't stop but hurries along no matter what when necessity spurs him on, so we filed into the gap—one behind the other, climbing the stairway so narrow that it separates all climbers.

And like the little stork that lifts its wing, wanting to fly, yet dares not leave the nest and lets the wing drop, so my wish to inquire kindled and quenched, and went so far as causing me to make the move of a man ready to speak.[2] Although our pace was swift, my dear father did not hold back, but said, "Go ahead and release the bow of speech that you have already drawn so far."

Then I confidently opened my mouth and asked, "How can one grow emaciated there where no one needs any food?"

"If you would recall how Meleager was consumed along with a branch in a fire, it wouldn't seem so puzzling.[3] And if you think of how your every movement

---

[1]This means that it was 2 p.m. in Purgatory.

[2]Storks used to symbolize obedience because the little ones allegedly waited for their mothers' permission before leaving the nest. John Ciardi assumes that Dante has just cleared his throat.

[3]Virgil points out that we accept many correspondences without puzzling over them. Meleager was a hero in Greek mythology who was fated to live no longer than it took the branch in his mother's fire to finish burning. Knowing this, she doused the branch and hid it away.

is matched by your image in the mirror, that which seems hard would seem easy to you. But to put your mind at rest, here's Statius, and I call upon him and pray him to soothe your distress."

"If I explain the eternal view of things in your presence," Statius answered him, "my excuse is that I can't say no to you."[4] Then he said, "Son, if you pay attention and accept my words, they will illumine your 'how?'.[5]

"Perfect blood, which is not drunk by the body's thirsty veins, but remains like leftover food to be removed from the table, in the heart acquires power to create someone else's body parts, just as the blood in the veins nourishes one's own body parts. Turned clear, it descends into that organ which is best unmentioned; and from there it eventually sprays onto someone's blood in the container provided by nature.[6]

"There the two are mingled—one passive, and the other active due to its perfect place of origin. So joined, the active blood goes to work, first coagulating and then

---

When Meleager eventually killed his two brothers, she took out the old branch and finished burning it, thus causing his death.

[4]Virgil and Statius are both able to answer Dante, but defer to each other courteously.

[5]Dante had asked how spirits with no need to eat could grow thin. What he gets is a medieval lecture, based upon teaching of Aristotle and Thomas Aquinas, about human reproduction and human psychophysiology. Statius undertakes to explain the nature of human procreation, embryology, ensoulment, and astral bodies.

[6]According to this theory, semen is especially pure male blood, destined to unite with female menstrual blood in the uterus. All generative power was assumed to be in the semen. According to Dorothy Sayers, "[this view] was almost universally accepted until very recent times, when it became possible to distinguish microscopically the action of genes in sperm and ovum. (Popular psychology and popular moral standards still remain surprisingly faithful to the scientific theory of the third century B.C.)"

enlivening the passive blood it has solidified. Once the active force has become a living entity like a plant (aside from the fact that a plant is fully developed and the human embryo is still in process), it manages to move and feel, rather like a sea-sponge. Then the active force sets about developing all the various parts for which it is the seed.[7]

"Now, son, the life force from the heart of the biological father swells and spreads, as nature concentrates on developing all its new parts. But you cannot see yet how it changes from an animal into a human being. That has caused one wiser than you to stumble, so that he taught that the intellect is separate from the human body, since he could not locate it in any body part.[8]

"Open your heart to the truth that is coming: understand that as soon as the brain is perfectly distinct in the fetus, the First Mover[9] turns to it with joy over nature's skill, and breathes into it a vigorous new spirit. That spirit draws into itself the activity of the fetus, making a human soul that lives, feels, and is self-aware. That you may be less bewildered, consider how the heat of the sun combines with the juice of the vine to make wine.[10]

---

[7]In scholastic teaching, there were three stages of human existence: (1) simple life, like that of a plant, (2) perceptive, feeling life, like that of an animal, and (3) reflective life, exclusively human. The first two stages can only receive impressions, but the third has the capacity for reasoning and conceptualizing.

[8]Because the functional abilities of animals unquestionably reside in the brain, the Spanish-Arabian philosopher Averroes reasoned that the power of human reason does not reside in the brain. Therefore, he taught that human intelligence is an eternal, universal quality which humans partake of only during their natural lives. The impersonal mind of humanity as a whole is immortal, according to Averroes, but no human souls are immortal. Of course Dante disagreed on this point.

[9]God.

[10]In referring to wine, Statius is offering a chemical analogy, not an explanation.

"And when Lachesis runs out of thread,[11] the soul separates from the body and carries away a person's full human and divine essence. Once the physical characteristics are muted and passive, however, the memory, intelligence and will are sharper and more active than ever. Lingering not, the soul falls miraculously of its own accord onto one of two shores; and there it first realizes what road it is taking.[12]

"As soon as the soul is enclosed in its new place, its formative power radiates as it did before to form the living body parts; and as watery air displays rainbow colors when sunbeams are reflected in it, so wherever the soul is located the nearby air takes on the appearance that the soul imprints upon it. Just as a flame follows the fire wherever it moves, so the spirit is followed by its airy new form.

"This visible form composed of air is called a shade, and it recreates for itself all the sense organs including sight. This is how we speak and laugh, and it is how we make the tears and groans you may have heard circling the mountain. The shade gets its appearance from our strong desires or other feelings; and that is the cause of your astonishment."[13]

---

[11] In Greek mythology, when the Fate named Lachesis runs out of thread , someone dies.

[12] Upon death every Hell-bound soul goes straight to the shore of Acheron, and every Heaven-bound soul goes to the shore of the Tiber.

[13] John Ciardi observes that although humans may appear virtuous by fraudulently hiding their evil desires, shades must appear on the outside as they are on the inside. Dorothy Sayers notes that what we call a shade in Hell or Purgatory is called a ghost if it appears on earth. The shade is only an interim appearance, and "must not, of course, be confused with the Body of Glory which will be assumed at the Resurrection, and which is a real, although (in St. Paul's words) a 'spiritual' body, with powers transcending those of the 'natural' body."

And now we came to the last turn of the stairs and bore to the right, and we were immediately absorbed in a new concern. There the mountainside belches forth flames, and a mighty updraft blasts the flames back, leaving only a narrow path along the outer rim of the ledge. We had to file forward along the rim one by one; I feared the flames on my left and the cliff on my right.

My Leader said, "Along here we must tightly rein our eyes, because a loose rein could easily cause a false step."

Then I heard "God of supreme clemency" sung in the heart of the conflagration, which did nothing to diminish my desire to look over there. I saw spirits moving through the flames, and so I watched them and also watched my steps, eyes darting back and forth. After the end of the hymn they called out "I know not a man" and softly began the hymn again.[14]

When the hymn was finished this time, they cried out, "Diana stayed in the woods and chased away Helice, who was poisoned by Venus."[15] Then they returned to their hymn; then called out the names of women and husbands who were as chaste as virtue and marriage require us to be. And I think this is all they have to do as long as the fire burns them; for with such a treatment and such nourishment their final wound must be healed.[16]

---

[14]"Summa Deus clementine" ("God of supreme clemency") is the opening of an old Latin hymn begging God to burn away lust and strengthen chastity. The words called out after the hymn, "Virum non cognosco," are Mary's statement of her virginity in the Latin translation of Luke 1:34.

[15]In classical mythology Diana stayed in the woods to preserve her virginity, but her unfortunate helper Helice succumbed to sexual desire and bore Jove a son.

[16]Dorothy Sayers explains, "Fire, which is an image of Lust, is also an image of Purity. The burning of the sin, and the burning of charity, which is its opposing virtue, here coalesce into a single image and a single experience."

CANTO TWENTY-SIX

A Fiery Path

While we were going thus along the edge, one ahead of the next, my good Master often said, "Take care, heed my warning!"

The sun's rays, which were already bleaching the western sky from blue to white,[1] were striking my right shoulder and casting my shadow upon the flames, making them redder. Many passing shades noticed that small detail and paid attention. That is what caused them to begin to discuss me, saying "He doesn't seem to be a shade." Then some of them approached me, as close as they could come while remaining careful not to step out where they would not be burned.

"You there, walking behind the others—probably because of respect rather than indifference—answer me, burning here with thirst and fire. Your answer is not for me alone; all these with me thirst for your answer more than an Indian or Ethiopian thirsts for cold water. Tell us how it is that you serve as a wall blocking the sun, as if you were not yet trapped in the net of death."

Thus one of them spoke to me, and I would have answered instantly if I hadn't been distracted by another strange thing that happened just then; for people were approaching in the middle of the burning path from the opposite direction, which made me stop and stare. There I see each shade quickly kiss one from the opposite group

---

[1]The sun always makes the clear sky closest to it look white rather than blue, and the sun is far in the west now because it is after 4 p.m.

without a moment's pause, satisfied with this brief greeting.[2] So it is that in their dark ranks one ant nuzzles another as if to get directions or to spread the news.

As soon as the friendly greeting ends, before their next footstep on the way, each tries to outshout the other: the newcomers, "Sodom and Gomorrah,"[3] and the others, "Pasiphaë enters the cow to attract the bull to her lust."[4]

Then like cranes flying off in two directions—some to the Rhipean mountains and others to desert sands, some avoiding the frost and others the sun[5]—one group heads one way and the other the other way, both tearfully singing and shouting appropriate praises.

The same ones who had entreated me drew close again, looking eager to listen. Seeing their desire for the second time, I said, "You souls who are sure of attaining peace

---

[2]Shades in Purgatory have all moved counter-clockwise until this group of homosexuals appeared, moving clockwise. The pure affection between the shades of lustful heterosexuals and lustful homosexuals is expressed in obedience to Romans 16:16, "Greet one another with a holy kiss."

[3]The homosexuals' call raises the terrible memory of Genesis 19:1-28, in which the evil men of Sodom were determined to rape two strangers who were visiting Lot. The visitors were actually angels, who saved Lot and then destroyed Sodom and the entire valley with burning sulfur. This happened circa 2000 B.C.

[4]According to Greek legend, in about 2000 B.C. Pasiphaë, the lustful wife of King Minos of Crete, hid inside an ingenious artificial cow (constructed of hides cleverly mounted on a frame) in order to experience mating with a bull. She was impregnated and gave birth to the monstrous Minotaur. Dante cites this as an example of perverted heterosexuality.

[5]The Rhipean mountains was a term referring to far northern Europe, and the term desert sands probably referred to Africa. Dante does not mean that cranes really fly off in two directions this way. He refers to cranes in order to echo the passage about lustful souls in Hell, described in Canto 5 of *The Inferno*: "As the cranes call out their laments while making a long streak of themselves across the sky, so I saw the spirits come, uttering wails, carried by the buffeting winds."

sooner or later, my limbs haven't been left over there, either young or old, but are here with me, with their blood and joints. I am traveling up through here in order to be blind no longer. There is a lady above who gained grace for me to carry my mortal body through your world.

"So that your deepest desires may soon be fulfilled and you may live in heaven, which is full of love and spread so wide—please tell me, so I may write it into my notes, who you are and who that crowd is, moving in the opposite direction."

Each shade resembled an astonished man of the mountains, rough and uncivilized, who is bewildered and stares around speechless when he ventures into the city. But when they got over their shock, which is soon calmed in noble hearts, the one who first questioned me said, "You are blessed, because in order to die a better death, you are now exploring our country. The people going the other direction sinned in the manner that once caused victorious Caesar to hear 'Queen' shouted at him.[6] That is why they call out 'Sodom,' upbraiding themselves, as you have heard, and their shame aids the fire that purifies them.

"Our sin was heterosexual; but because we broke human law and followed our lust like brute beasts, when we leave the others we recite in self-rebuke the name of her who bestialized herself in the disguise of a beast.[7]

---

[6]Caesar's relations with the King of Bithynia earned him the nickname "Queen of Bithynia," and when he defeated Gaul his jubilant soldiers sang about the affair to mock him—in the spirit of what is today called a *roast*.

[7]Their sin was that of wrongly joining the opposite sex in violation of the human law of right and wrong. All normal human beings in all times and places are imprinted with this Natural Law, which is the basis for all ethics and morals. As Dorothy Sayers notes, "The popular misuse of the phrase 'Natural Law' to connote the 'laws of Nature' is inaccurate and misleading and should be strongly discouraged." The

"Now you know our deeds and what we were guilty
of; but if by chance you want to know our names, there is
not time to tell them all, and I don't know them anyway.
I'll make short work of your curiosity about me, however;
I am Guido Guinicelli, cleansed this far already because I
repented before I died."[8]

Like the two sons who beheld their mother again after
the ragings of Lycurgus (although I do not rise to their
actions),[9] so I felt when I heard him identify himself as
father to me and others superior to me who always used
sweet, gracious rhymes of love. Struck deaf and dumb
and lost in thought, I walked along staring at him for a
long time. Because of the fire, I couldn't get closer. When I
had my fill of staring, I eagerly pledged him my service
with convincing vows.

He said, "What you say makes such a vivid
impression on me that Lethe can't wash it away or make
it dim.[10] But if your words swore to the truth just now,
tell me why you show in speech and looks that you hold
me so dear."

I answered, "Your sweet verses, which so long as
current usage lasts, shall make the very ink that wrote
them precious."

"Brother," he said, "the one I am pointing out with my
finger" (and he pointed to a spirit ahead of us) "was a

Natural Law is uniquely human, and some of the behaviors that are
innocent in animals are sinful in human beings. For a superb
description of the Natural Law, see *The Abolition of Man* by C. S. Lewis.

[8] The outstanding Italian poet Guido Guinicelli had been dead only
24 years in 1300.

[9] In Statius's *Thebaid*, the twin sons of Hypsipyle arrived just in time
to embrace her and save her from execution at the hands of King
Lycurgus. Dante feared fire and did not try to embrace Guido because
of the flames that surrounded him.

[10] Lethe is the mythical river of forgetfulness.

better wordsmith of our mother tongue.[11] He surpassed
everyone who wrote love verses and prose romances; and
let fools say that the one from Limoges is best.[12] They
judge by common talk rather than by truth, and make up
their minds without taking time to hear about art and
reason. That's what many of our fathers did with
Guittone, voice after voice declaring him the champion —
but then at last most saw the truth.[13]

"Now if you have the great privilege of being permitted
to go up to the monastery where Christ is head of the
assemblage,[14] say the Lord's Prayer there for me — so far
as it is applicable to us in this world where the power to
sin is gone."[15] Then perhaps to give someone behind him
his space, he vanished through the flames like a fish
swimming through the water to the bottom.

I drew myself forward toward the person he had
pointed out and said that my desire was preparing a
place of welcome for his name. He answered willingly,
"Thy courteous request doth please me so that I cannot
and will not hide from thee. I am Arnaut, who weeps and
goes singing. In grief I see my former folly; in joy I see the
day I look for that is coming. Now I pray thee by the

---

[11] Arnaut Daniel was a famous troubadour who wrote in his native
Provençal, a language which rather resembles French.

[12] Guirant de Bornelh had a more popular style and in his day was
called "master of the troubadours."

[13] Guido d'Arezzo, called Guittone, was a fine scholar as well as an
admirable reformer who preached religion and peace, according to
Dorothy Sayers; but his verse tended to be less than first-rate.

[14] Heaven.

[15] The lines "Lead us not into temptation, but deliver us from evil"
are no longer an appropriate prayer for people in Purgatory because
they are forever safe from temptation and evil.

Goodness that guides thee to the top of the stairway, that in due time thou might remember my pain."[16]

---

[16] Arnaut Daniel's words are cast here in slightly antiquated English to indicate the fact that Dante actually wrote them in Daniel's Provençal rather than Italian. Arnaut is asking Dante to hasten his progress toward heaven by praying for him.

CANTO TWENTY-SEVEN

Through a Wall of Flame

Just as it is when the sun sheds his first beams there where his Creator shed his blood, while Spain lies beneath the constellation of Libra, and Ganges' waves are scorched by noonday heat—so here the day was passing away when God's glad angel appeared to us. He was standing outside the flames on the bank and singing "Blessed are the pure" in a voice beyond all mortal music.[1]

"Blessed souls, you cannot go any farther until the fire bites you first; go on in and don't be deaf to the singing beyond," he said to us when we drew close to him; and when I heard him say this, I felt like someone laid in the grave. I bent forward over my clasped hands, gazing at the fire and picturing the human bodies I had seen burnt.[2]

My kind escorts turned to me, and Virgil said, "My son, this may mean suffering, but not death. Remember, remember... If I guided you safely on Geryon, what shall I do now nearer to God?[3] Believe me, if you stayed a thousand years in the middle of these flames, they could not burn one hair of your head; and if by chance you think

---

[1] This is the angel of chastity, and he is singing *"Beati mundo corde,"* Matthew 5: 8 in Latin translation.

[2] Anyone who ascends this high must pass through the wall of fire before going on. Dante had probably seen people burned at the stake. In any case, both he and his sons were condemned to be burned at the stake if they ever returned to their beloved Florence; therefore, year after year he had resisted his yearning to return.

[3] In *The Inferno*, Canto 17, Dante was afraid to ride on Geryon, and on their downward ride he saw fires and heard the cries of sufferers.

I am deceiving you, get close to the flames and hold out the edge of your hem to check. Leave behind now, leave behind your fear; turn to the fire, and come in confidently."

But I wouldn't budge, in spite of my conscience. When he saw me obstinately rooted to the spot, he was a bit perplexed and said, "Now look, son, this wall stands between Beatrice and you." As dying Pyramus opened his eyes at Thisbe's name and gazed at her the day the mulberry became red, so when I heard the name which is always springing up in my mind my firmness melted and I turned to my wise guide.[4]

At that he shook his head and said, "Well, do we want to stay on this side?" and smiled as one does to a child that is won over by an apple. Then he entered into the fire in front of me, asking Statius, who had been walking between us for a long time, to come behind me.

Once I was inside, I would have thrown myself into molten glass to cool off, the heat was so immeasurably intense. My gentle father went on talking about Beatrice to encourage me, saying, "I seem to behold her eyes already."

A voice singing on the other side of the fire guided us through, and by concentrating on it we emerged where the ascent began. "Come, ye blessed of my Father" rang out from within a light which was so bright it overwhelmed me and I couldn't look at it.[5] "The sun is sinking," it

---

[4]In the legend referred to here, Pyramus thought his lover Thisbe was dead and stabbed himself beside a mulberry tree. Thisbe arrived, and when he heard her say her name Pyramus revived enough to open his eyes. Then he died, she killed herself, and mulberries have been red ever since in honor of their tragic love.

[5]The complete quotation, "Then shall the King say unto them on his right hand, Come, ye blessed of my Father, inherit the kingdom prepared for you from the foundation of the world," is Matthew 25:34. Dante heard it in Latin, *"Vesite benedicti patris mei."* (This verse comes

added, "and evening is coming; don't linger here, but hurry along before the west grows dark."

Our way led straight up through the rock, and on the path ahead my body blocked the rays of the setting sun. After a few steps we knew the sun had set behind us, because my shadow ahead had vanished. Before the vast horizon had become all one color and night held everything in her dominion, each of us used a step for a bed; for the law of the Mount took from us the power and desire to climb higher.

Like goats that have been nimble and frisky on the heights before they are fed, but afterward grow tame while ruminating quietly in the shade out of the hot sun as the herder guards them, leaning on his staff—and like the herder who stays outside watching all night over his flock lest a wild beast attack—such were all three of us then, I like a goat and they like herders, bounded on both sides by high rock walls.

Little of the sky could be seen there, but through that narrow view the stars grew bigger and brighter than usual. As I was drifting mentally and gazing at them, sleep fell on me, sleep which often gives us news before it happens. I think it was the hour when Venus, who seems to be always aflame with love, first beamed upon the mountain from the east, when in my dream I seemed to see a fair young woman in a meadow gathering flowers and singing: "Whoever wants to know my name, know that I am Leah, working with my lovely hands to make myself a garland to enjoy in my reflection in the mirror. But my sister Rachel never stirs from her mirror, and sits there all day. She prefers to gaze into her own bright eyes, as I

---

after the parable of the sheep and the goats.) At this point the final P has been erased from Dante's forehead.

prefer to adorn myself with my hands. She finds joy in seeing; I find it in doing."[6]

And now, at the brightness before sunrise (so welcome to returning travelers who spend each night closer to home), the shadows were fleeing on every side and my sleep fled with them; so I arose, seeing that the great teachers had already risen.

"Today the sweet fruit that mortals seek on so many trees will satisfy all your hungerings with peace." These are the words Virgil said to me, and it was the sweetest news I ever heard. So greatly did waves of desire to ascend surge over me that at every step I felt my feet grow wings.

When all the stairway was below us and we were on the topmost step, Virgil fixed his eyes on me and said, "Son, you have seen the temporal fire and the eternal fire and have reached the place where I, myself, discern the way no farther. I have brought you here with my intellect and art; now let your pleasure be your guide. You are past the steep paths, past the narrow paths.[7]

"See how the sun shines on your brow; see the tender grass, the flowers, and the shrubs that grow here of their own volition. You can rest or walk among them while the

---

[6]The sisters Leah and Rachel were Jacob's two wives described in Genesis 29. Leah, who had weak eyes, bore him more children; but Rachel, who was more beautiful, was his favorite. Like Martha and Mary in the New Testament, the active sister produced more good works, but the function of the contemplative sister was even more valuable. Dante is obviously like both, but more like Martha because he was extremely active and productive by nature. In my opinion his gathering of materials and weaving them together to produce the *Comedy* is intentionally reflected in Leah's gathering flowers and weaving them together to produce a garland.

[7]Dante has seen the destructive fires of Hell and the purifying fires of Purgatory. Now that he has safely reached this entryway to Paradise, he needs Virgil as his guide no longer. This is the ending of the main part of *Purgatory*.

glad fair eyes are coming, the eyes that were weeping when they made me come to you. No longer expect words or signs from me. Your will is free, upright and whole, and it would be wrong not to act according to its prompting; therefore I crown and mitre you over yourself."[8]

---

[8]The imperial crown and papal mitre symbolize government and religious authority. Virgil means that now that Dante's soul has been purified and he is entering heaven, he needs no more institutional authorities, governmental or religious, because his soul is directly attuned to God. Dante has arrived at the transcendent Garden of Eden at the top og Mount Purgatory. As Dorothy Sayers comments, the widespread myth of a Golden Age has been inspired by a universal spiritual homesickness for Paradise, a kind of racial memory of the Garden of Eden.

Terrestrial Paradise.
Gustave Doré (Canto 28)

CANTO TWENTY-EIGHT

The Sacred Wood

Eager now to explore within and around the holy, dense, and verdant forest which was filtering the morning light, without any more delay I left the stairway, moving over the tableland with lingering step, over the ground which breathed out fragrance everywhere.[1]

A sweet, steady breeze stroked my face gently, before which the branches, responsively trembling, were all swayed in the direction in which the morning shadows were being cast on that holy mountain.[2] But they were not bent enough to disturb the little birds in the treetops that were practicing their art; for with their song full of gladness they welcomed the early breezes into the midst of leaves which were murmuring with the burden of their songs—just like the sound that gathers from bough to bough through the pine wood on Chiassi's shore when Aeolus sets Sirocco free.[3]

---

[1]This sacred wood is our race's original Paradise. It is the opposite of the dark wood where Dante began his journey in Canto 1 of *The Inferno*. But as Dorothy Sayers points out, the innocence of this lost paradise was never mankind's ultimate destiny; it was the starting point, and the goal was always the spiritual perfection of heavenly paradise.

[2]The breeze blew from east to west, and the shadows cast by the morning sun fell from east to west.

[3]Dante is describing the beautiful pine forest of Ravenna on the Adriatic coast. (He lived in Ravenna when he wrote this.) Since Dante's time the shore receded from Ravenna, leaving it far inland; in the twentieth century the remaining forest was extremely damaged by the

My slow steps had already carried me so far into the ancient wood that I could no longer see where I had entered, and then a stream blocked my path; its little splashing waves bent to the left the grass on its banks. All the waters that are purest on earth would seem somewhat polluted compared with that water, which hides nothing although it flows darkly beneath everlasting shade which never lets the sun or moonlight through.

My feet stopped, but my eyes went on beyond the stream to gaze at the array of fresh blossoms there; and suddenly there appeared to me (the way something appears so suddenly that it cancels all other thoughts) a solitary woman who wandered along singing and gathering flower after flower from those that painted her path with color.[4]

"Pray, fair lady, you who sun yourself in love-beams (if I may believe outward looks, which often show what's in the heart), may it please you to come forward," I said to her, "toward this stream, so I can understand what you are singing. You remind me of Proserpine the day her mother lost her and she lost the spring flowers."[5]

As a female dancer turns around with feet close to the ground and to each other and barely puts one foot before the other, so she turned toward me upon the little red and yellow flowerets, the way a virgin drops her modest eyes; and she satisfied my prayers, drawing so near that I could

---

two world wars. Aeolus was mythical king of the winds, and the Sirocco blows into Italy from the southeast.

[4]In Canto 33 Dante will reveal that the woman's name is Matilda. Because of his recent precognitive dream, it is evident that Matilda represents the active side of religious life. Historically, she may possibly represent Matelda, the Grancontessa of Tuscany (1046–1115), who was a generous benefactor of the Church. Her role in the story is to prepare Dante for his meeting with Beatrice.

[5]Demeter's lovely daughter Proserpine was abducted by Pluto, king of the underworld, while she was gathering flowers one day.

hear the meaning of her sweet sound. As soon as she was where the grass is lightly splashed by the waves of the fair river, she generously raised her eyes to me. I do not believe so bright a light could have shone beneath the eyelids of Venus when she was accidentally pierced by her son.[6]

She smiled from the far bank while she went on gathering more of the flowers that this high land bears without seed. The river kept us three steps apart; and the Hellespont, where Xerxes crossed (to this day a rebuke to all human pride), bore no more hatred from Leander for its turbulence between Sestos and Abydos than this one did from me because the waters didn't part.[7]

"You are newcomers," she began, "and perhaps you are mystified because I am smiling in this place that is the nest of the human race; but the psalm Delectasti provides light that may uncloud your understanding.[8] And you in front, who entreated me, speak if there is anything else you want to hear; I am prepared to answer your questions until you are satisfied."[9]

"The water," I answered, "and the murmuring of the forest contradict some information I received recently."[10]

---

[6]When playful Cupid accidentally scratched his mother Venus with a dart, she instantly fell in love with a mortal named Adonis.

[7]King Xerxes of Persia (485–465 B.C.) proudly crossed the Hellespont (the modern Dardanelles) to invade Greece with a million soldiers; but he crossed back in a fishing boat after most of his soldiers perished. Leander swam across the Hellespont many times to visit Hero, his lover; but he was eventually drowned on the way.

[8]Psalm 92:4 says "For thou, Lord, hast made me glad through thy work: I will triumph in the works of thy hands." As Dorothy Sayers observed, the widespread idea that holy places must be solemn places is an error.

[9]For the first time, Dante has been walking ahead of his two companions and taking the lead.

[10]Statius informed Dante that above St. Peter's Gate there is no more atmospheric disturbance (see Canto 21), but Dante sees flowing water (evidence of rain) and hears a light wind.

To this she answered, "I will tell what causes your surprise, and I will clear away the mist that bothers you. The Highest Good, whose joy is Himself, made man good and for goodness, and gave this place to him as a foretaste of eternal peace. Through his own fault he lived here only briefly; through his own fault he exchanged spontaneous laughter and sweet play for tears and labor.

"Below this mountain, vapors from the water and the earth which rise in heat brew atmospheric turbulence. To protect people who come here, this mountain rose so high that it is free of these forces. Now because the upper atmosphere revolves around the earth with its original motion, unless its circuit is impeded in some way it brushes steadily across this mountaintop. That movement makes a sound in the wood because of its density; and the procreative energy of plants can impregnate this universal breeze, which then scatters seed abroad; and the land below, according to its suitability and climate, conceives and brings forth a variety of trees of various kinds. If this were understood, it would not seem marvelous when some plant takes root there without any known source of seed. And you must know that the holy highland where you are is full of every seed and bears fruit which is not harvested on earth below.

"The water which you see does not well up from a spring fed by moisture which cold condenses, like a river that gains and loses volume, but issues from a sure and constant fountain which regains by God's will just as much as it pours forth freely on either side. On this side it flows down with power to cleanse the human memory of sin; on the other it restores the memory of every good deed. It is called Lethe on this side and Eunoë on the other, and it won't work unless both sides are tasted. This water excels all other flavors.

"And although your thirst may be fully satisfied without my revealing any more, I will give you a bonus as a favor; I doubt that my words will be less welcome to you if they exceed my promise. Those who in olden times sang of a Golden Age and its happy state, perhaps in their Parnassus were dreaming of this place.[11] Here the root of the human race was innocent; here spring is everlasting, with every kind of fruit; this water is the nectar the poets wrote about."[12]

Then I turned around and looked back at my poets and saw that they had heard the last explanation with smiles; and so I turned to face the fair lady again.[13]

---

[11] Parnasus was the place of poetic inspiration.

[12] As Dorothy Sayers comments, the widespread myth of a Golden Age has been inspired by a universal spiritual homesickness for paradise, a kind of racial memory of the Garden of Eden.

[13] For an explanation of how Sandro Botticelli depicted key features of Cantos 28-31 in his allegorical painting "Primavera," see the essay "Botticelli's Primavera and Dante's *Purgatory*" on p. ix.

Charity, Hope, and Faith
Gustave Doré (Canto 29)

CANTO TWENTY-NINE

Seven Golden Candlesticks

Although her speech was finished, like a woman in love she burst into song: "Blessed are they whose sins are covered."[1]

Like nymphs who used to walk singly through woodland shadows (one desiring to enjoy, another to avoid the sun), she then advanced upstream along the bank, and I kept abreast of her, matching small steps to her dainty steps.[2] After fewer than a hundred steps, the parallel banks made a bend that turned me toward the cradle of the day.[3] We hadn't gone very far this way when the lady faced me, saying "My brother, look and listen."[4]

---

[1] Psalm 32:1 in the Latin Vulgate, "*Beati quorum tecta sunt peccata.*"

[2] In Canto 12 Dante had matched his steps to those of the artist Oderisi, bent low under the crushing weight of his old pride. Now he matches his steps to those of a joyful spirit instead.

[3] Because 100 stood for perfection, Dante composed the *Comedy* of 100 cantos. Fewer than 100 steps probably means 99 steps (3 times 33). The cradle of the day is the East, and facing the sunrise traditionally symbolizes turning toward God.

[4] Beginning with the news from Matilda that he must be observant, Dante's experience in Canto 29 loosely reflects the experience of John in Revelation 4. For the reader's convenience, that chapter is included here in the New International Version:

After this I looked, and there before me was a door standing open in heaven. And the voice I had first heard speaking to me like a trumpet said, "Come up here, and I will show you what must take place after this."

At once I was in the Spirit, and there before me was a throne in heaven with someone sitting on it.

I saw such a sudden radiance flash through the great forest that I thought it might be lightning. But since lightning ends as fast as it begins, and this light continued, growing brighter, in my mind I said "What can this be?" A sweet melody ran through the luminous air; and a corresponding wave of indignation caused me to condemn the recklessness of Eve, who, alone and inexperienced in this place where heaven and earth obeyed God, was unwilling to wear her veil of obedience under which, if she had been faithful, I would have enjoyed these indescribable delights far earlier and longer.

While I moved on through these first-fruits of eternal pleasure, entranced and yearning for more, under the

---

And the one who sat there had the appearance of jasper and carnelian. A rainbow, resembling an emerald, encircled the throne.

Surrounding the throne were twenty-four other thrones, and seated on them were twenty-four elders. They were dressed in white and had crowns of gold on their heads.

From the throne came flashes of lightning, rumblings and peals of thunder. Before the throne, seven lamps were blazing. These are the seven spirits of God.

Also before the throne there was what looked like a sea of glass, clear as crystal. In the center, around the throne, were four living creatures, and they were covered with eyes, in front and in back.

The first living creature was like a lion, the second was like an ox, the third had a face like a man, the fourth was like a flying eagle.

Each of the four living creatures had six wings and was covered with eyes all around, even under his wings. Day and night they never stop saying: "Holy, holy, holy is the Lord God Almighty, who was, and is, and is to come."

Whenever the living creatures give glory, honor and thanks to him who sits on the throne and who lives for ever and ever, the twenty-four elders fall down before him who sits on the throne, and worship him who lives for ever and ever. They lay their crowns before the throne and say:

"You are worthy, our Lord and God, to receive glory and honor and power, for you created all things, and by your will they were created and have their being."

green boughs ahead of us the air seemed to blaze and the sweet sound was clearly the chanting of a choir. O holy, holy maidens, if I have ever endured fasting, cold, or vigils for you, now I crave my reward. Now is the time for Helicon to overflow for me and for Urania to aid me with her choir to write in verse things hard to comprehend.[5]

A little way ahead we seemed to see seven trees of gold, but that false appearance was caused by the intervening space; when I had drawn so close that the similarity to trees was not increased by distance, the mental ability that makes sense of things recognized them for what they were, candlesticks,[6] and the words of the chant for what they were, "Hosannah!"[7]

Above, a light show was flaming forth, far brighter than the full moon in a clear midnight sky. Full of

---

[5]Helicon was the mountain sacred to the muses, and Urania was the muse of astronomy and heavenly things. Dante is invoking the muses to help him with his story.

Dante is going to try to describe an amazing heavenly pageant that was performed for his benefit. According to Dorothy Sayers, this pageant is in the general form of a Corpus Christi procession in honor of the Blessed Sacrament. In a sense the pageant is even harder for readers to comprehend today than in Dante's day because of modern unfamiliarity with this kind of pageantry and extended allegory.

[6]In Dante's time, seven processional torches were widely used at the Bishop's Mass, evidently based upon Revelation 1:12-13, "And being turned, I saw seven golden candlesticks ..." Although I am not aware of any other commentator considering this possibility, in my opinion the seven candelabras represent the seven days of creation. Creation is God's original, universal revelation, preceding the books of the Bible, as declared by Paul in Romans 1:20 (NIV): "For since the creation of the world God's invisible qualities—his eternal power and divine nature—have been clearly seen, being understood from what has been made, so that men are without excuse." Revelation 4, the basis of Canto 29, ends with the same general theme.

[7]Hosannah means "Save, we pray." This is what the crowd shouted to Christ at his triumphal entry to Jerusalem (see Matthew 21:9), and this procession is indeed a kind of triumphal entry.

wonderment I turned to my good Virgil, but he looked back with a face as bewildered as mine. Then I turned again to the extraordinary things that moved toward us so slowly that even newly-wedded brides are quicker.[8]

The lady cried to me, "Why are you so excited about seeing these brilliant lights, but not about what comes after them?" Then I beheld people following the lights, dressed in white—whiteness beyond any seen on earth. The water on my left was shining brightly, and it reflected my left side like a mirror.

When I had positioned myself on my side of the river so that only the water separated me from the procession, I stayed in place to see well and watched the flames advance, streaking the air behind them with bands of color like trailing pennants; so that the air above remained streaked with seven bands in the colors of the rainbow and Delia's sash. These banners streamed back farther than I could see, and I estimate that the outer ones were ten paces apart.[9]

Beneath the streaked sky that I've described, along came twenty-four elders, two by two, crowned with wreaths of lilies. They were singing, "You are blessed

---

[8]This procession is slower than a stately bridal procession. At this point in the story it is obvious that Dante may encounter Beatrice at last.

[9]Delia's (Diana's) sash is a term for the halo around the moon, which Dante links to the rainbow. The high visibility of the rainbow seems to tally with the streaks of colored light in the sky and Paul's claim in Romans that God's qualities are clearly seen in his creation. According to Dorothy Sayers, two visionary Bible passages that refer to the rainbow, Ezekiel 1:28 and Revelation 4:3, provide the imagery for this entire pageant. Most commentators believe the seven streaks in the sky stand for seven aspects of God's Spirit listed in Dante's *Convivio*: wisdom, understanding, counsel, power, knowledge, piety, and the fear of the Lord. (Six of these qualities are listed in Isaiah 11:2.) Others say the seven streaks stand for seven gifts of the Holy Spirit.

among the daughters of Adam, and may your beauties be blessed eternally."[10]

When the flowers and tender herbs on the opposite bank were relieved of those chosen people, four creatures came next (just as star follows star in the sky), each one crowned with green leaves.[11] Each had six wings, full of eyes; and the eyes of Argus, if he were living, would be like those.[12] To describe the four, reader, I can spare no more poetry, for I'm obliged to tell so much more that I can't be lavish here. But read Ezekiel, who depicts them as he saw them coming from the frigid North, with whirlwind, cloud, and fire; and as you find them in his pages, so they were, except for the wings. On that subject John agrees with me, rather than Ezekiel.[13]

The space in the midst of the four of them contained a triumphal chariot with two wheels, harnessed to the neck of a Griffin.[14] His wings stretched up into the streamers of colored light and neatly bracketed the middle one, leaving the outer three on either side so that no streamer was

---

[10]The elders (referred to in Revelation 4:6-8) here are like actors that play the parts of the books of the Old Testament (counted in a condensed way by Jerome), and their song that echoes words spoken to Mary in the first chapter of Luke implies that the Old Testament is a preparation for the Incarnation.

[11]Green leaves symbolize hope.

[12]In Greek mythology Argus was a monster with a hundred eyes, and his eyes were transferred to the tail of a peacock. The eyes symbolize knowledge of past and future.

[13]Dante's creatures look like the four living creatures in Ezekiel 1:4-14 and 10:8-14, but each has six wings instead of four, like the four Beasts of the Apocalypse in Revelation 4:6-8. They represent the four evangelists, Matthew, Mark, Luke, and John.

[14]The chariot, which is much like a moving throne, represents the real Church, which will be triumphant. Instead of riding in it, the Griffin is pulling it.

interrupted.[15] The wings soared on up out of sight; the part that was a bird was gold, and the rest was white mingled with blood red.[16] Not Africanus, or even Augustus, ever gladdened Rome with such an elegant chariot;[17] even the chariot of the sun would look poor beside it, the one that was incinerated by Jove's inscrutable justice because of earth's pious prayers when it went off course.[18]

Three maidens moved forward, dancing in a circle by the right wheel; one so red she would hardly be visible in a fire; the next as green as if her flesh and bone were made of emerald; the third like new-fallen snow. Now the white one seemed to lead the dance, and now the red; and from the red one's song the others paced their dance slowly or quickly.[19]

---

[15]It has been suggested that the wings of the Griffin represent mercy and justice, referring to Psalm 36: "O stretch forth thy mercy over those that know thee, and thy justice over them that are of a right heart."

[16]The Griffin has the head and wings of an eagle and the body of a lion, representing the dual nature of Christ, who is both God and man. The gold of the eagle symbolizes Christ's divinity, and the white and red symbolize his humanity. Of the latter, the white symbolizes Christ's purity, and the red symbolizes his passion. (White can also stand for justice and red for love, and so white represents the Old Testament, and blood red represents the New Testament.) Dante probably had in mind Song of Solomon 5:10-11, "My beloved is white and ruddy, the chiefest among ten thousand. His head is as the most fine gold ..."

[17]Scipio Africanus and Caesar Augustus rode on jeweled chariots after their victories.

[18]The story of Phaeton's disastrous adventure was cited in *The Inferno*, Canto 17. Jove killed Phaeton with a thunderbolt because he was driving his father's chariot so recklessly that it looked as if he were going to set the earth on fire. Allen Mandelbaum suggests that Dante may have tied Phaeton's misuse of that chariot to the misuse of the Church by some of its leaders.

[19]The white dancer is faith, the green dancer is hope, and the red dancer is charity (love). As Paul said in his letter to the Corinthians, the

By the left wheel, four more maidens were dancing in purple costumes, led by one who had three eyes.[20]

After all these, I saw two aged men, dressed differently but alike in gravity and dignity. One seemed to be a disciple of Hippocrates, whom nature made to help her favorite creatures.[21] The other showed the opposite intention; his sword was glittering and sharp, and even on my side of the stream I feared it.[22]

Next I saw four men with humble appearance.[23] Behind all these came a solitary old man, moving like a sleepwalker but with keen intelligence in his face.[24] And these seven men were dressed like the twenty-four elders, but they had no wreaths of liles on their heads. Instead, they wore roses and other red flowers; one who viewed

---

greatest of these is charity. (These three colors are central to the pageant, and they also happen to be the colors of the Italian flag.)

[20] These are the four cardinal virtues: prudence, justice, temperance, and fortitude. They wear purple, designating royalty. ((It has been reported that *purple* used to mean very dark red rather than reddish blue.) Prudence has a third eye in her forehead, symbolizing her wisdom about the past, present and future.

[21] Nature's favorite creatures are human beings.

[22] Hippocrates was a great medical pioneer. The two aged men represent Luke, the doctor called "the beloved physician" in Colossians 4:14, and Paul, whose traditional emblem is a sword (his "Sword of the Spirit" is the Word of God). Because the participants in the procession represent the books of the Bible, and the Gospel of Luke has already been represented by one of the four winged creatures, the first aged man must represent Luke's Book of Acts. The man with the sword represents all the Pauline epistles.

[23] The humble four represent minor epistles by James, Peter, John, and Jude. Some say the red flowers on their heads represent martyrdom.

[24] The solitary last man represents the last book in the Bible, Revelation, which is uniquely prophetic and symbolic; it describes truths experienced in a vision or a dream.

them from a distance would have sworn they were aflame above the eyes.[25]

When the chariot was straight across from me, a thunder clap sounded; further progress seemed to be prohibited, and the worthy characters simultaneously halted there behind the archetype at the front of the procession.[26]

---

[25]The wreaths on the heads of these allegorical figures have allegorical significance. White lilies represent the righteousness of the Old Testament, green leaves represent the hope of the Gospel, and red roses represent the love of the New Testament.

[26]The entire procession, from blazing candlesticks to the elderly sleepwalker, halted simultaneously for Dante.

CANTO THIRTY

From a Cloud of Flowers

When the seven-starred constellation of heaven (never
setting or rising, never obscured by any mist but sin, and
showing everyone his duty, just as the lower sky's seven-
starred constellation guides a mariner into port)[1] stopped
still, the truthful group between that constellation and the
Griffin turned to the chariot as if it were their peace; and
one of them, like an announcer from heaven, chanted three
times "Come, bride of Lebanon," and all the others echoed
him.[2]

---

[1]The "seven-starred constellation of heaven" means the seven huge
candlesticks that guide the righteous, just as the seven stars of the sky
guide navigators back to their port. Some commentators think Dante
was referring to the Big Dipper, and others think he was referring to the
Little Dipper. There is no doubt that he borrowed the image of seven
stars from Revelation 1:16, 20; 2:1. and 3:1. ("In his right hand he held
seven stars, and out of his mouth came a sharp double-edged sword.
His face was like the sun shining in all its brilliance." "The mystery of
the seven stars that you saw in my right hand and of the seven golden
lampstands is this: The seven stars are the angels of the seven churches,
and the seven lampstands are the seven churches." "To the angel of the
church in Ephesus write: These are the words of him who holds the
seven stars in his right hand and walks among the seven golden
lampstands." "To the angel of the church in Sardis write: These are the
words of him who holds the seven spirits of God and the seven stars...")

[2]The twenty-four elders are standing between the Candelabras and
the Griffin. The elder who represents the books of Solomon sings aloud
three times the words of Song of Solomon 4:8 in the Latin Vulgate,
"Veni, sponsa de Libano." This bride may represent the individual soul

As at the last trumpet every saint will spring from his grave with his newly restored voice singing Hallelujah, so it was now that a hundred ministers and messengers of eternal life rose up on the divine chariot at the voice of such a great elder, proclaiming "Blessed art thou that comest" and, tossing flowers high and low, "Oh, with full hands give lilies."[3]

Oftentimes at daybreak I have seen the eastern part of the sky flushed and rosy, and the rest of it a clear, pale blue; and the face of the sun came up so veiled in mists that the eye could behold it a long time. So it was that within clouds of flowers flung from angelic hands and falling down on and around the chariot, a woman appeared to me crowned with a wreath of olive branches over a white veil, wearing a green cape over a gown the color of living flame.[4] And my spirit—that had gone so long since it had been stunned with awe, trembling in her presence—now without a better look at her instantly succumbed again to the power of her presence, staggered by the impact of that old, old love.

As soon as that force struck me which had first hit me while I was still a boy, I turned to my left (with the trust with which a little child runs to his mother when he is frightened or pained) to say to Virgil: "Less than a drop of blood is left in me that doesn't tremble; I recognize the embers of the ancient flame."[5]

---

intended for union with God, the Church as a whole, and the Virgin Mary.

[3] A hundred angels responded to the elder's announcement with a cascade of flowers and two cries in Latin, *"Benedictus qui venis"* (Matthew 21:9, Mark 11:9, Luke 29:38, and John 12:13) and *"Manibus O date lilia plenis"* (from Virgil's *Aeneid*).

[4] The woman who is greeted by the angels is Beatrice. She is wearing the colors of faith (white), hope (green), and charity (red).

[5] Dante's words are quoted from Virgil's *Aeneid*.

But Virgil had left us bereft of himself—Virgil, dear father, Virgil to whom I totally entrusted myself! And all that our first mother lost could not hold back my tears from covering my cheeks so recently washed with dew.[6]

"Dante, don't weep about Virgil leaving, don't weep yet—because you are soon going to have much more to weep about." Just as an admiral out on the stern or bow looks at the crews that man the other ships and encourages their brave deeds, so on the left side of the chariot, when I turned at the sound of my name (which I'm forced to mention here), I saw the lady who had appeared half-veiled beneath the angelic celebration, looking across the stream at me.[7]

Although the veil which fell from her head, crowned with Minerva's leaves, did not completely reveal her, yet she appeared stern and regal.[8] She continued, like a speaker who holds back the hottest words till last, "Look at me well; I am indeed, I am Beatrice. How did you dare to come to this mountaintop?[9] Didn't you know that people are happy here?"

---

[6]Dante wept in spite of the beauties of the Forest of Eden and in spite of his memory of Virgil washing away all sorrowful tear stains from his face at the bottom of Mount Purgatory.

[7]This is the only place in the *Comedy* where Dante mentions his own name. He thought it was poor style for an author to mention his own name unnecessarily. But he must have realized that his disclaimer would draw attention to his name.

[8]The olive was sacred to Minerva, Goddess of Wisdom. Beatrice evidently represents spiritual wisdom.

[9]Beatrice may be reminding Dante that through her efforts on his behalf Virgil brought him this far in spite of his faithlessness, foolishness and fear. In *The Faith of Dante Alighieri* (p. 55) Geoffrey Nuttall admitted he found the following passage deeply offensive. "Our first reaction may well be, 'If, after all this, this is what Beatrice is going to be like, I shall read no more.' For years these cantos were so offensive to me that I could not bear to read the *Purgatorio* to the end again. Then I began to realize that so deliberate an artist as Dante could

I dropped my eyes to the clear stream; but seeing my reflection there, I drew them back to the grassy bank because I was so weighed down by shame. Much like a mother who seems harsh to her child, so she seemed to me; for tough love has a bitter taste.

She was through, and immediately the angels sang "In thee, O Lord, do I put my trust," but beyond "my feet" they did not go.[10]

As the snow on the living rafters along Italy's spine is frozen hard in blasts of Slavonian wind, then melts and trickles down through itself like candlewax melting in flame if the land without noontime shade breathes on it,[11] I was without tears or sighs until the song of those whose notes blend with the melodies of the eternal spheres. But when I heard in their sweet harmonies their compassion for me, as if they had said "Lady, why do you shame him so?" the ice which had closed about my heart became breath and water, and with anguish gushed out through my mouth and eyes.[12]

She, still standing on the left side of the chariot, then spoke to the compassionate angels: "You live in an everlasting day, so that neither night nor sleep steals from you one step the world may take along its way; but I

---

not conceivably be unaware how objectionable to the reader this cold douche was sure to be; and then, that he must have forced himself to describe what for him personally was so humiliating, only because it was true. I found that without it I could not go on with him into Heaven."

[10]See Psalm 31:1-8, "In thee, O Lord, do I put my trust... thou hast set my feet in a large room." From the Latin Vulgate Dante quoted the words "*In te, Domine, speravi,*" and "*pedes meos.*" (Dante's feet are set now in the spacious Forest of Eden.)

[11]These lines describe the snow on the ridges of the Apennines when the winds blow from the north. The living rafters are tree limbs. The snow melts when warm breezes blow from Africa.

[12]Dorothy Sayers considered this emotion the turning point of Dante's journey through Purgatory.

must speak with great care so he who weeps may understand me, in order for his sorrow to match his sin.

"Not only by operation of the mighty spheres that direct each seed to its destination according to the stars, but by bounties of divine grace which rain down from clouds so high we cannot see them, this man had so much potential in his youth that any of his talents could have yielded a wonderful harvest. But the better the soil, the wilder the crop becomes with bad seed and neglect.

"For a while I upheld him with my countenance; with my youthful eyes I led him along toward righteousness. But as soon as I was on the threshold of adulthood and changing to a different stage of life, he forsook me and gave himself to others.

"When I was risen from flesh to spirit, and my beauty and goodness were increased, I was less precious and less pleasing to him than before. He turned his steps toward wrong paths, pursuing false visions of good and false promises. My various inspirations didn't help, with which in dreams and other ways I called him back, because he paid so little attention to them. He sank so low that the only means left for his salvation was showing him the people who are lost.

"For this I visited the portal of the dead and, weeping, requested help from the one who has guided him up this far. God's high decree would be broken if he crossed Lethe and drank of it without shedding tears of penitence."

Beatrice
Gustave Doré (Canto 30)

CANTO THIRTY-ONE

Plunged into the Holy Stream

"You there, on the other side of the holy stream," she began again (I had found the edge of her conversation sharp enough, but now she thrust the sharp point into me), continuing without delay, "Say, say if this is true or not; to such an accusation you must add a confession."

I was so dumbfounded that when my voice began to speak it died in my throat. She waited briefly, then said, "What are you thinking? Answer me, for your sad memories are not yet washed away."

Confusion and terror, mixed together, forced from my mouth a "Yes" so soft that it required lip-reading. As a cross-bow snaps both string and bow when pulled too hard, and the bolt hits the target ineffectively, so I snapped under her hard rebuke, releasing a torrent of tears and sobs that drowned my voice.[1]

Then she said, "In your desire for me that caused you to love ultimate goodness, what chains or trenches did you find across your path that caused you to abandon hope of moving ahead?[2] And what allurements or benefits

---

[1] Dorothy Sayers explains that now that Dante has acquired a state of innocence, he is overwhelmed by the hideousness of his own past sin. As long as his nature retained the slightest trace of sin, he didn't see sin this clearly.

[2] The ultimate goodness is God, and the image of the Creator sometimes appears to people in his creatures. Dante loved the manifestation of God that he encountered in Beatrice.

did you perceive in other faces to cause you to strut around before them instead?"[3]

After heaving a bitter sigh, I barely found a voice to answer with, and with difficulty my lips managed to shape my words. Weeping, I answered, "Temporary things with their false attractions turned my steps aside as soon as your face was hidden."

Then she said, "If you were silent, or if you had denied what you have confessed, your guilt would not be any less obvious; your Judge knows everything. But in our Court when self-accusation bursts from a person's mouth, the grindstone is turned back against the blade's edge.[4] Nevertheless, in order for you to feel more ashamed of your error and to be stronger when you hear the Sirens next time, stop sowing tears and listen; you will hear how my buried flesh should have moved you toward a different goal.

"Neither nature nor art ever delighted you as much as the lovely body that contained me, now scattered in dust; and if my death destroyed your heart's delight, how could anything transitory capture your heart again? Surely, at the first arrow of that kind you should have winged upward to me, no longer mortal. No young girl or other passing fancy should have weighed down your wings to await capture. The fledgling waits for two or three arrows; but in the presence of the fully-feathered bird, the net is spread or arrow shot in vain ."

---

[3]In *The Faith of Dante Alighieri* (p. 54) Geoffrey Nuttall explains, "At a first reading we think Beatrice is just jealous and inexcusably so. We know Dante well, and he is not as bad as all that! ...The bitter experience to which Beatrice now exposes him comes as the towering consummation of [his spiritual education in Purgatory]. ...To enter Heaven forgiven, even temporarily and still only by special grace, as he is to do, he must know the same cleansing tears of a repentance genuinely his own."

[4]Confession blunts the edge of the Sword of Justice.

As a tongue-tied, shame-faced child hangs his head repentantly during a scolding, so I did. And she continued, "Since listening has made you grieve, lift up your beard so that looking will make you grieve more."

A sturdy oak is less resistant to uprooting, whether by our wind or wind that blows from Iarbas' land,[5] than my head was when I lifted my face at her command; I understood well the venom of her words when she called my face my beard.[6] And when my face was lifted, my eyes made out the primal creatures now at rest that had been scattering flowers; and then, not yet entirely clear, they saw Beatrice turned toward the Beast that is one person with two natures. Even under her veil and beyond the stream, she seemed to surpass her former self in beauty as much as she used to surpass all other women.

The thorns of repentance stung me so that the very things I used to love most became most disgusting to me. So much remorse gnawed at my heart that I fainted, and the one who caused it knows what happened to me then. When at last my heart restored me to consciousness, I saw above me the lady I had found alone; and she urged, "Hold on! Hold on!"

She plunged me into the river up to my neck, and, pulling me after her, crossed over the water, light as a boat.[7] When I was close to the blessed bank I heard *"Asperges me"* so sweetly sung that I cannot remember it, much less describe it.[8]

---

[5] One wind blows from the north of Europe (Italy's continent), and the other blows from Africa, here called "Iarbas' land" after a Libyan king with that name.

[6] Beatrice sarcastically reminds Dante that he is a grown man, not a little bird or a naughty child.

[7] The lady walks across the water.

[8] The *Asperges* is sung when a priest sprinkles people with holy water at the beginning of the Mass. The text is Psalm 51:7, "Purge me

The lovely lady opened her arms, clasped my head, and immersed me so that I had to swallow water. Then she pulled me out and led me, washed clean, into the dance of the four fair ones; and each of them raised her arms over me. "Here we are nymphs and in the sky we are stars; before Beatrice descended to the world we were given to her as her handmaids.[9] We will lead you to her eyes; but the three over there on the other side, who see more deeply, will help to sharpen your eyes to see inside her joyous light."

Thus they chanted; and then they led me up to the Griffin's breast, where Beatrice stood facing us. They said: "Look well, so you won't stint your eyes; we have placed you before the emeralds where Love once aimed his arrows at you."[10]

A thousand desires hotter than flame held my eyes bound to her shining eyes, which remained fixed upon the Griffin. Like the sun caught in a mirror, the twofold Beast was beaming within them, now with the attributes of one, now of the other nature. Imagine, reader, if I was amazed or not when I saw something remain motionless while its reflected image kept changing.[11]

---

with hyssop, and I shall be clean: wash me, and I shall be whiter than snow."

[9] The Four Cardinal Virtues, Justice, Prudence, Fortitude, and Temperance, first appeared to Dante as stars when he arrived at the base of Mount Purgatory. According to Dorothy Sayers, they are the best that humanity can achieve without the revelation of Christ's Church, and they were ordained to be the handmaidens of the Church before it was founded.

[10] The eyes of Beatrice were shining like jewels, but it is not clear whether Dante meant that they were green (the color of hope) or not.

[11] This is Dante's first beatific vision of the nature of Christ, as the lion (human) and the eagle (divine). He sees it by staring into the eyes of Beatrice (the Church).

While my soul, filled with wonder and gladness, was tasting of that food which both satisfies and increases hunger, the other three, whose bearing showed them to be of higher rank, drew forward while dancing to the beat of their angelic roundelay.[12] "Turn, Beatrice, turn your holy eyes," was their song, "to your faithful follower who has come so far to see you. Out of your grace do us the grace, unveil your mouth to him that he may discern the second hidden beauty."[13]

O splendor of eternal living light, what poet has ever grown so pale in the shade of Parnassus or drunk so deeply at its spring that he would not seem to have his mind confounded on trying to describe your appearance when in the free air you unveiled yourself there where heaven's harmony is reflected in your face!

---

[12]Dante has tasted love, and in theological terms he has tasted Christ. These three are the Theological Virtues, Faith, Hope, and Charity.

[13]Dante finds inner beauty most fully evident in the eyes and the mouth. Although this judgment is understandable as a fact of human physiognomy, it can also be taken allegorically: inner beauty is most manifest in what one perceives (sees with one's eyes) and what one expresses (says with one's lips).

CANTO THIRTY-TWO

The Tree of Knowledge

My eyes were so fixed and intent on satisfying their ten years' thirst that all my other senses went numb; and my eyes had blinders of indifference on both sides because that holy smile had captured them in her net as she used to do. But I was forced to glance toward the left when I heard the three goddesses warn me, "You stare too fixedly." And as it often happens if we look at the sun, I was blinded by the light a little while.[1]

When my eyes adjusted to the dimness (dimness in contrast to that from which I had to turn away), I realized that the glorious army had wheeled to the right to face the east, heading back toward the sun with the seven flames leading the way.[2] As under its shields an advance troop turns to retreat, and their flag moves on before the rest of the army has finished turning, so the advance soldiers of the heavenly kingdom passed by us before the chariot had turned its pole-shaft.[3] Then the ladies returned to their

---

[1]This canto moves from Dante's ecstatic contemplation of Beatrice's face to the hideous desecration of the Church. It is the longest canto in the entire *Comedy*.

[2]The first part of the Biblical pageant is over. Now Dante and Statius will join the procession and walk to what could be called the second act.

[3]The military analogy is appropriate here because this part of the pageant is about the war between good and evil. The advance troops were the 24 elders representing the books of the Old Testament. The pole-shaft by which the Griffin pulls the chariot represents the cross, by which Christ saves the Church.

places by the chariot wheels, and the Griffin pulled its blessed burden in such a way that not a feather was ruffled.

The fair lady who had pulled me across the river and Statius and I walked by the wheel that made the smaller arc.[4] So we passed through the tall forest (emptied by the one who believed the serpent), and a melody of angels matched the rhythm of our steps. We had advanced perhaps as far as three flights of an arrow when Beatrice descended from the chariot.

I heard everyone murmur "Adam!"[5] Then they surrounded a tree stripped bare of leaves and flowers on every bough. Its branches spread wider the higher it rose, and its height would amaze even the residents of India.[6]

"Blessed are you, Griffin, that with your beak you do not pluck sweet fruit from this tree, forbidden because it tortures the belly afterward."[7] So the others cried around the sturdy tree.

And the Beast with two natures answered, "Thus is preserved the seed of all righteousness."[8] And having turned to the pole-shaft which he had been pulling, he

---

[4]The right wheel made the smaller arc when the chariot turned to the right.

[5]They have arrived at the Tree of Knowledge of Good and Evil, which in its barren state represents the sin of Adam. They murmur his name in disapproval of his sin.

[6]In Dante's time many Europeans believed there were extremely tall trees in India.

[7]See Romans 5:12: "Wherefore, as by one man sin entered into the world, and death by sin, and so death passed upon all men for that all have sinned."

[8]According to John Gallagher in *To Hell and Back with Dante*, the words of the Griffin are a paraphrase of Matthew 3:15, "...it is proper for us to do this to fulfill all righteousness" (NIV).

dragged it to the foot of the barren tree. And he tied what came from that tree to the tree forever.[9]

As our trees swell with buds when sunlight falls to earth along with the starlight that shines after the fish constellation, before the sun harnesses his team beneath the next constellation—just as our trees burst into foliage and each is decked again in color, so this tree with naked boughs renewed itself, blossoming into a tint less than rose and more than violet.[10]

I did not understand the hymn the people sang (it is not sung on earth), and I didn't hear it to the end. If I could describe how the pitiless eyes, whose long guard duty cost so much, fell asleep during the story about Syrinx—then like a painter who paints from a model I would show how I fell asleep; let such an artist portray drowsiness.[11] Therefore I skip ahead to when I awoke; I saw a radiance that ripped away the veil of my sleep, along with the call "Arise! What are you doing?"[12]

---

[9]There is an old legend that Christ died on a cross made of wood from the Tree of Knowledge of Good and Evil, which bore the forbidden fruit.

[10]In Italy deciduous trees bud and burst into bloom when the Aries constellation replaces the Pisces constellation (from late March to late April). When the pole-shaft (representing the cross) is tied to the tree of Adam, it suddenly bursts into full spring bloom. (C. S. Lewis echoed this miracle in *The Lion, the Witch and the Wardrobe*.) The color of the blossoms, between rose and violet, probably means some pale shade of purple like that of lilacs or jacaranda.

[11]Juno sent Argus, who had a hundred eyes, to guard a girl loved by Jupiter. Then Jupiter sent Mercury to trick him. Mercury lulled Argus to sleep by telling him a series of stories about Syrinx, then cut off his head.

[12]Dante awakens to behold what could be called the third act of the instructive pageant. The Griffin and the elders are gone (Christ has ascended, and the books of the Bible are complete), and the Church will be under attack from without and within.

Just as Peter and John and James were brought to see the blossoms of the apple tree which makes the angels long for its fruit and provides a perpetual marriage feast in heaven[13] —just as they were overcome by it and came to themselves at the word by which greater slumbers had been broken,[14] and then they saw their band diminished by Moses and Elijah and saw their Master's garment transformed,[15] even so I came to myself and saw that tender one bending over me, the one who had guided my steps along the stream.[16]

All perplexed, I asked "Where is Beatrice?" She answered, "See her sitting on the tree root below the new foliage. See the companions that surround her; the others

---

[13]See Song of Solomon 2:3, "As the apple tree among the trees of the wood, so is my beloved among the sons. I sat down under his shadow with great delight, and his fruit was sweet to my taste." This is allegorically interpreted as Christ.

[14]The word "Arise" roused Lazarus from the slumber of death. See John 11.

[15]The transfiguration witnessed by Peter, James and John was a foretaste of heaven, just as appleblossoms are a foretaste of the fruit. See Matthew 17:1—8, "And after six days Jesus taketh Peter, James and John his brother, and bringeth them up into an high mountain apart, and was transfigured before them: and his face did shine as the sun, and his raiment was white as the light, and, behold, there appeared unto them Moses and Elias talking with him. Then answered Peter and said unto Jesus, Lord, it is good for us to be here: if thou wilt, let us make here three tabernacles; one for thee, and one for Moses, and one for Elias. While he yet spake, behold, a bright cloud overshadowed them, and behold a voice out of the cloud, which said, This is my beloved Son, in whom I am well pleased; hear ye him. And when the disciples heard it, they fell on their face, and were sore afraid. And Jesus came and touched them, and said, Arise, and be not afraid. And when they had lifted up their eyes, they saw no man, save Jesus only." Dante likens himself to Peter, James and John because he, too, was overpowered by God's revelation, and he, too, obeyed the command "Arise."

[16]Matilda is taking care of Dante.

are mounting up after the Griffin with sweeter and deeper song."

And I don't know if her words continued after that because now before my eyes was the one who had usurped all my attention. She sat alone on the bare earth, left there as guardian of the chariot which I had seen the two-natured Beast tie fast. The seven nymphs formed a protective ring around her, with lights in their hands that are secure from northern and southern winds.[17]

Beatrice said, "You shall be a visitor here for a short time, but throughout eternity with me you shall be a citizen of that Rome of which Christ is a Roman.[18] Therefore, to help the world that lives badly, fix your eyes on the chariot and be sure that when you return to earth you write down what you see." So I, a willing slave to her commands, focused my mind and eyes where she directed.

When it falls from the highest part of the sky, lightning has never descended from dense clouds as swiftly as I saw Jove's bird swoop down through the tree, ripping away its bark and flowers and new leaves; and he hit the chariot with all his might.[19] At that it reeled like a boat in a storm, beaten by the waves, now to starboard, now to port. Then I saw a half-starved she-fox leap into the body of the triumphal vehicle. Rebuking her for foul sins, my

---

[17] Now the seven Virtues are holding the seven candelabras.

[18] This part of the pageant is about the first millennium of Christendom, which was seated in Rome. But Beatrice is promising Dante an eternity with her in Christ's true city, which is heaven. Dante may have had in mind Ephesians 2:19, "Consequently, you are no longer foreigners and aliens, but fellow citizens with God's people and members of God's household" (NIV).

[19] An eagle was the emblem of Rome, and this allegorical attack represents the persecution of the early church by Roman emperors from 64 to 314 A.D.

lady made her flee as fast as her bare bones could carry her.[20]

Then through the tree I saw the eagle plunge into the body of the chariot and leave it feathered with his plumage.[21] And as a voice comes from a sorrowing heart, such a voice came from heaven and said, "O my little boat, you are loaded with evil!"[22]

Then it seemed to me that the earth opened between the two wheels, and I saw a dragon emerge that drove his tail up through the chariot. Like a wasp that retracts its stinger, by withdrawing its poison tail it wrenched out part of the bottom and slinked away.[23]

That which remained, like good land overgrown with weeds, covered itself with the feathers that might have been donated with good intentions. In the time it takes to open the mouth to utter a groan, the pole-shaft and both wheels were completely covered by them.[24]

Thus transformed, the sacred vehicle sprouted heads— three over the pole-shaft and one at each corner. The first three had two horns, like an ox; but each of the other four

---

[20]The fox represents various heresies in the early Church that temporarily threatened its future.

[21]The second attack of the eagle, which penetrated the Church, was the well-intentioned but disastrous wealth and status conferred on the Church by the first Christian emperor, Constantine. The feathers represent compromise and corruption.

[22]The sad voice is considered to be that of Peter, who was a fisherman.

[23]Although the dragon has often been identified as Satan, it probably represents Islam, which arose in the sixth century and pulled away part of the Church. Dante probably drew the image of the dragon from Revelation 12:3, "his tail drew the third part of the stars of heaven and did cast them to earth."

[24]The corruption of the Church (caused by wealth and power) became rampant.

had a single horn on its forehead. Such a strange monster has never been seen before.[25]

Seated upon it, secure as a fortress on a steep hill, I saw a loosely dressed whore with eyes that darted greedily.[26] I saw that a giant who seemed to be in charge of her stood at her side, and from time to time they kissed each other.[27] But when she turned her lustful and insolent eyes to me, her brutal lover beat her from head to toe.[28] Then, filled with jealousy and cruel with rage, he untied the monster and dragged it into the wood, hiding the monster and the whore from my sight.[29]

---

[25]The chariot has been transformed into a monster with seven heads and ten horns. (See the description of the Beast of the Apocalypse in Revelation 17:3, "...and I saw a woman sitting on a scarlet colored beast full of the names of blasphemy, having seven heads and ten horns.") John Ciardi interprets the seven heads as the seven deadly sins. The first three are pride, wrath, and avarice. The other four are sloth, envy, gluttony, and lust. One of the other theories about the seven heads is that they represent the seven hills of Rome.

[26]The whore represents the corrupt papacy in Dante's day.

[27]The giant is the French monarchy in Dante's day, which was notorious for its intrigues with the popes.

[28]The whore's obvious desire to get away from the giant, and the price she paid for it, probably represent Pope Boniface's unsuccessful attempts to distance himself from the power of Nicholas the Fair of France and align himself with various Italian rulers. The attempts ended in military defeat in 1303.

[29]The giant's removal of the corrupt Church from Dante's presence most likely represents King Philip's arrangement with a French pope, Clement V, that moved the Papal See away from Italy to Avignon, France, in 1309. That relocation gave Philip complete control over the Church.

CANTO THIRTY-THREE

A Holy Spring

"O God, the heathen are come" is the psalm the weeping women's choir gently began, alternating between the group of three and the group of four.[1] While Beatrice listened, sighing with compassion, she changed almost as much as Mary changed at the cross. But when the seven virgins paused and she could speak, up she stood and answered fierily "'A little while, and ye shall not see me,' my beloved sisters, 'a little while, and ye shall see me'."[2]

Then she placed the seven in front of her, and with a nod she motioned the lady and the remaining sage and me to come behind her.[3] Thus she moved ahead, and I don't think her tenth step had touched the ground when her eyes struck my eyes; and with tranquillity she said to me,

---

[1]See Psalm 70:9, "O God, the heathen are come into thine inheritance; thy holy temple have they defiled; they have laid Jerusalem on heaps." Dante quoted the beginning from the Latin Vulgate, *"Deus, venerunt gentes."*

[2]See John 16:16, Christ's assurance to his disciples: "A little while, and ye shall not see me; and again, a little while, and ye shall see me, because I go to the Father." Dante quoted from the Latin Vulgate, *"Modicun, et non videbitis me, et iterum... Modicun, et videbitis me..."* Dante did not live to see the return of the Medieval Church to Rome that he predicted through Beatrice's assurance to her companions; it occurred in 1377.

[3]The lady is Matilda, and the remaining sage is Statius. (Virgil has left.)

"Come faster, so that if I speak with you, you will be close enough to listen to me."[4]

As soon as I was with her, as it was my duty to be, she said to me, "My brother, why don't you question me as we move along?"

I was like those in the presence of their betters who don't speak up and are so deferential they can't get their full voice to their lips. With faltering voice I began, "My Lady, you know what I need to know and what is good for me."

She answered, "I want you to disentangle yourself now from fear and shame so you no longer speak like one who's half awake. Know that the vessel the dragon broke was, but is not; let the one to blame find out that God's vengeance respects no evasions.[5] The eagle that left feathers on the chariot, turning it into a monster and then a prey, will not remain without heirs.[6] For I definitely see (and therefore declare) that approaching stars, impervious to any resistance or interference, will bring us times in which a five-hundred ten and five, sent by God, will kill the whore along with that giant who sins with her.[7]

---

[4]Beatrice had taken nine steps forward when she invited Dante to come closer. Numbers had allegorical significance to Dante, and he repeatedly relates the number nine (three times three) to Beatrice.

[5]In his *Purgatory* commentary Henry Wadsworth Longfellow noted, "In the olden time in Florence, if an assassin could contrive to eat a sop of bread and wine at the grave of the murdered man, within nine days after the murder, he was free from the vengeance of the family, and to prevent this they kept watch at the tomb. There is no evading the vengeance of God in this way. Such is the interpretation of this passage by all the old commentators."

[6]The eagle is the Roman Empire, and Dante believed that the last legitimate emperor was Frederick II, who died in 1250.

[7]The meaning of 515 will probably never be settled, but Dorothy Sayers was convinced that it stood for the person Dante called "the Greyhound" (see the first canto of *The Inferno*), often identified as Cangrande Della Scala (1291-1329). Some interpreters note that by

"Perhaps my prophecy won't convince you, because it is as obscure as those of Themis and the Sphinx; all such prophecies hide their meaning. But soon the facts themselves will be the Naiads that solve this hard riddle, without loss of grain or flocks.[8]

"Listen carefully! Exactly as I say these words, so you must report them to those living the life that is a race toward death. And when you write them down, be sure not to omit how you have seen the tree twice ruined here.[9] Whoever robs it or tears it with a blasphemous act offends God, who created it holy for his sole use. Because of eating its fruit, the first soul suffered in torment and desire for over five thousand years, yearning for Him who has Himself paid for that bite.[10]

---

transcribing the clue in Roman numerals and rearranging them, one gets the word DUX (*duce*), meaning "leader." Allen Mandelbaum considers Emperor Henry VII (1274-1313) the most likely possibility. Whoever Dante had in mind, he expected that man to radically reform the corrupt Church.

[8]The Sphinx used to defeat men with her riddle about the animal that walks on four feet in the morning, two feet at noon, and three feet in the evening. Oedipus came up with the solution: mankind crawls in infancy, walks in maturity, and leans on a cane in old age. Themis was an oracle who sent a wild beast to damage the herds and fields of the Thebans. Unfortunately, many people used to be misled by a textual error that seemed to attribute the solution of the Sphinx's riddle to the Naiads, who had nothing to do with it. If Dante had not been misled, he would have said that unfolding events would be the Oedipus (rather than the Naiads) to solve the riddle of 515.

[9]The tree was first ruined by Adam's sin, and later ruined by the persecution and corruption of the church.

[10]Dante was following the chronology of the historian Eusebius, who figured that more than 5,000 years passed between Adam's expulsion from the Garden of Eden and the crucifixion. At the time of the crucifixion, Adam was rescued by the Harrowing of Hell.

"Your intellect is asleep if it hasn't perceived the reason for that tree to be so tall and so full at the top.[11] And if your idle thoughts had not been like the River Elsa to your mind, and their pleasantness like Pyramus to the mulberry, by these facts alone you would have recognized the justice of God's prohibition.[12]

"But because I see your mind calcified and stonelike, so darkened that the light of my word dazes you, I want you to take my words away inside you—if not written out, at least outlined—for the same reason that the pilgrim's staff is brought back decked with palm."[13]

I answered, "As wax receives a permanent imprint from a signet ring, my brain is now imprinted by you.[14] But why do your long-awaited words soar so far beyond my grasp that the harder I try, the less I understand?"

"So you can judge," she said, "that school of thought you followed, and see how well its teaching keeps pace with my word; so you can see how far your way is from the divine way—as far as the highest and swiftest heaven is from the earth."[15]

---

[11] The tree that represents God's knowledge of good and evil soars beyond the reach of human understanding.

[12] The Elsa is a river in Tuscany with chemical properties that create a mineral crust on anything soaked in that water. The blood of Pyramus permanently stained mulberries a dark red color.

[13] According to Dorothy Sayers, Beatrice wants Dante to carry home at least the images of the pageant, if not the interpretation. Pilgrims to the Holy Land used to decorate their walking sticks with palm fronds to show where they had been.

[14] Geoffrey Nuttall has pointed out that Dante's experience with Beatrice has brought to a climax what went on for him all through Purgatory.

[15] Beatrice is probably referring to Dante's study of human philosophy, which proved inadequate for understanding spiritual truths. He should have trusted less in earthbound human reason and more in divine love.

Therefore I answered her, "I don't remember ever turning away from you, and I don't have such a lapse gnawing at my conscience."

"If you can't remember it," she smiled, "recall how you drank from Lethe today; if smoke is evidence of fire, this forgetfulness is evidence that your will was flawed and went astray. But from now on my words will be naked, as required by your weak perception."

More incandescent now, with slower steps, the sun was riding along the meridian which moves from place to place, when those seven ladies suddenly halted — just as a guide halts with his group if he finds the presence or possibility of something unusual — at the edge of a pale shadow like one cast over cool streams in the Alps, beneath green leaves and dark boughs.[16]

In front of them I seemed to behold the Tigris and Euphrates rivers welling up from one spring and parting like friends who linger.[17] "O light and glory of mankind, what water is this, springing from one source and then separating into two directions?"

In answer to my plea, I was told, "Ask Matilda to tell you."

Like one who wants to absolve herself of blame, that fair lady said, "I told him this among other things, and I am sure it wasn't Lethe's water that made him forget about it."[18]

---

[16]The sun seems brightest and slowest at noon. The noon meridian changes latitude with the seasons, but it is always noon at some longitude around the earth.

[17]The Tigris and Euphrates were two of the four rivers that flowed from the Garden of Eden according to Genesis 2:14. Dante probably had in mind a line from Boethius in *The Consolation of Philosophy* that mentioned their flowing from one spring.

[18]Lethe's water only washes away memories of sins and shortcomings, and Matilda's instruction was a good memory, not a bad one.

Beatrice answered, "Perhaps a greater concern weakens his memory and dims his perception, as often happens. But see Eunoë, which flows there; lead him to it, and in your customary way refresh his fading vitality."[19]

Like a gentle soul that makes no excuse and at the first sign of another's wish makes it her own, so the lovely lady set forth with me; and to Statius she said with womanly grace, "Come with him."

Dear reader, if I had more space for writing I would sing, at least in part, of that sweet drink which could never be too much; but since all the pages reserved for this second canticle are filled, art's roadblock lets me go no farther.[20]

I came back from the most holy waters born again, like trees renewed with new foliage; now I was pure and prepared to rise to the stars.[21]

---

[19]Dorothy Sayers perceives Beatrice's reference to Dante's "greater care" as a light-hearted hint that his memory lapse has been caused by his awe of her. In Sayers' opinion Matilda was one of Beatrice's girlhood friends in Florence, probably one who shared her gentle amusement about Dante. Matilda seems to serve all who reach the Forest of Eden by causing them to drink from the rivers of Lethe and Eunoë.

[20]Dante has arrived at the end of Canto 33 and won't spoil the careful symmetry of his epic by extending this part. (Of course, he could have saved room for this description if he had wanted to include it.)

[21]Each of the three books of the *Comedy* ends with the word stars. As C. S. Lewis explains vividly in his essay "Imagination and Thought in the Middle Ages," modern man feels that he is looking out from a warm, light place into the dark, cold desolation of space. But medieval man felt that we are now on the outside, looking "in" at the distant stars.

Epilogue

If readers of the *Comedy* began with the *Purgatorio* instead of the *Inferno*, there might be more of them. I confess that it is the Canzone I know best and love most (though I must add that, when I go on into *Paradiso*, I feel nothing else in the world is worth reading).

--Geoffrey F. Nuttall, *The Faith of Dante Alighieri*

FURTHER READING ON
PURGATORY

For readable translations of Purgatory into poetry, with helpful notes, I recommend the following:

Dorothy Sayers, *The Comedy of Dante Alighieri: Purgatory* (New York: Penguin Books, 1955). The second of three volumes, written in terza rima.

John Ciardi, *Dante Alighieri: The Purgatorio* (New York: New American Library, 1961). The second of three volumes, written in three-line rhymed stanzas. Ciardi prefaced this volume by saying, "Obviously no sane translator can allow himself to dream of success. He asks only for the best possible failure."

Allen Mandelbaum, *The Divine Comedy of Dante Alighieri: Purgatorio* (Berkeley, California: University of California Press, 1982). The second of three volumes, written in unrhymed verse without stanzas, with the Italian on the adjoining page.

For widely contrasting studies of Purgatory, I recommend:

C. S. Lewis, "Dante's Statius," *Studies in Medieval and Renaissance Literature* (Cambridge: Cambridge University Press, 1966). Lewis first published this essay in *Medium Aevum* in 1957. He examines and justifies the major role Dante gives to the Latin poet Publius Papinius Statius (c. 45-96 A. D.), who joins Dante in Canto 21 of Purgatory and accompanies him to the end of Canto 33.

Dorothy Sayers, "The Meaning of Purgatory," *Introductory Papers on Dante* (New York: Barnes & Noble, 1969).

Charles S. Singleton, *Purgatorio. 2. Commentary,* Bollingen Series LXXX, (Princeton, New Jersey: Princeton University Press, 1973.) An 850-page volume of line-by-line notes about *Purgatory* by one of America's leading Dante scholars. Most suitable for those who read *Purgatory* in the Italian.

Daniel Berrigan, *The Discipline of the Mountain:: Dante's Purgatorio in a Nuclear World,* A Crossroad Book (New York: Seabury Press, 1979). A free poetic adaptation of parts of *Purgatory* interspersed with warm prose reflections relating Dante's moral themes to contemporary American social issues. Berrigan, a prominent Jesuit priest, declares "What Virgil was to Dante, Dante became for me."

For general introductions to The Divine Comedy that are especially enlightening in regard to Purgatory, I recommend:

Charles Williams, *The Figure of Beatrice: A Study in Dante* (London: Faber & Faber, 1943). This intellectually passionate study of the writings of Dante is largely about the nature of romantic adoration. Williams focuses on the Way of Affirmation of images, the image of Beatrice, and the image of the City. He likens *The Divine Comedy* to Wordsworth's *Prelude.*

Dorothy Sayers, "On Telling You a Story" in *Essays Presented to Charles Williams,* edited by C. S. Lewis (Oxford: Oxford University Press, 1947). This extraordinary 37-page essay celebrates Sayers' discovery of *The Divine Comedy* in 1943 after reading *The Figure of Beatrice* by her friend Charles Williams. Unlike Williams, she shares her bubbling enthusiasm with ordinary readers and leads them into the pleasures of reading Dante.

C. S. Lewis, "Imagination and Thought in the Middle Ages" in *Studies in Medieval and Renaissance Literature* (Cambridge: Cambridge University Press, 1966). Lewis read this essay in two parts to a group of scientists at the Zoological Laboratory in Cambridge on July 17 and 18, 1956. In it he explains the sophisticated (not primitive) model of the universe that Dante and educated men of his day took for granted.

Geoffrey F. Nuttall, *The Faith of Dante Alighieri* (London: S.P.C.K., 1969). A series of four memorial addresses delivered at the University College of Wales in 1968: "The Poet and His Purpose," "Heaven and Hell," "Heaven's Antechamber," and "Heaven." "Heaven's Antechamber" is about *Purgatory*, Nuttall's favorite part of *The Divine Comedy*. These essays are warm, readable, and almost devotional.

Alan Jones, *The Soul's Journey: Exploring the Three Passages of the Spiritual Life with Dante as a Guide* (San Francisco: HarperSanFrancisco, 1995). A pastoral guide to spiritual growth by the dean of San Francisco's Grace Cathedral (Episcopal). The central section is titled "Purgatory" and includes three chapters: "Conversion: Recovering the Path to One's True Self," "Recovering the Path to Mutuality," and "Recovering the Vision of God." Jones writes, "Dante makes me feel and think, not only about the state of my soul, but about how I should vote."